REVELATION

REVELATION

EVERYDAY BIBLE COMMENTARY

Charles C. Ryrie

MOODY PUBLISHERS

CHICAGO

All Scripture quotations, unless otherwise indicated, are taken from the New American Standard Bible®, Copyright © 1960, 1962, 1963, 1968, 1971, 1972, 1973, 1975, 1977, 1995 by The Lockman Foundation. Used by permission. (www .Lockman.org)

Scripture quotations marked KJV are taken from the King James Version.

Cover design: Faceout Studio
Interior design: Smartt Guys design
Cover illustration of leaf pattern copyright © 2018 by Markovka / Shutterstock (74663932). All rights reserved.
Cover illustration of open book copyright © 2018 by IhorZigor / Shutterstock (185667422). All rights reserved.

Library of Congress Cataloging-in-Publication Data

Names: Ryrie, Charles Caldwell, 1925-2016, author.
Title: Revelation / Charles C. Ryrie.
Description: Chicago : Moody Publishers, 2018. | Series: Everyday Bible
    commentary series | Originally published: c1996. | Includes
    bibliographical references.
Identifiers: LCCN 2018010187 (print) | LCCN 2018012600 (ebook) | ISBN
    9780802497284 (ebook) | ISBN 9780802418258
Subjects: LCSH: Bible. Revelation--Commentaries.
Classification: LCC BS2825.52 (ebook) | LCC BS2825.52 .R97 2018 (print) |
DDC
    228/.07--dc23
LC record available at https://lccn.loc.gov/2018010187

ISBN: 978-0-8024-1825-8

We hope you enjoy this book from Moody Publishers. Our goal is to provide high-quality, thought-provoking books and products that connect truth to your real needs and challenges. For more information on other books and products written and produced from a biblical perspective, go to www.moodypublishers.com or write to:

Moody Publishers
820 N. LaSalle Boulevard
Chicago, IL 60610

1 3 5 7 9 10 8 6 4 2

Printed in the United States of America

CONTENTS

PUBLISHER'S NOTE

For over sixty years, the Everyday Bible Commentary series (formerly titled Everyman's Bible Commentary series) has served millions of readers, helping them to grow in their understanding of both God and His Word. These commentaries—written by a host of evangelical scholars who are experts in their respective fields—provide biblical interpretation that is both accessible and rich, impacting the daily lives of Christians from diverse cultural and theological backgrounds.

So why rerelease the Everyday Bible Commentary series given its immense success? These commentaries have served readers tremendously well in generations past, and we want to ensure that they serve many more for generations to come. While these commentaries are not new, they remain relevant as the content in each volume provides timeless scriptural exposition. And perhaps today more than ever, Christians need reliable biblical instruction that has stood the test of time. With so many voices vying for our attention and allegiance, Christians need to understand the voice of the One calling out to us in Scripture so we may faithfully live for Him and His glory. And it is to this end that these commentaries were written: that believers may encounter God through His Word and embody it in their everyday lives.

List of Illustrations

INTRODUCTION TO REVELATION

IMPORTANCE OF THE BOOK

Each book of the Bible is important, but the last book has the added significance of being the consummation and climax of God's revelation. The book of Revelation is especially significant because it concerns "things which must soon take place." We would not know many of these things if the book of Revelation were not in the Bible. It is the major (but not the only) prophetic book in the New Testament. John was commanded not to seal the book (22:10), and those who read it are promised a special blessing (1:3). Apparently, therefore, the book was expected to be understandable and helpful to those who read it. It is an apocalypse (literally, a revelation), designed not to mystify but to clarify.

AUTHOR AND DATE

According to the book itself, the author's name was John (1:4, 9; 22:8), who was a prophet (22:9). He was a leader in the churches of Asia Minor (chaps. 2–3) and was one of the earliest disciples of the Lord. He was the son of Zebedee, and his family were prosperous fishermen (Matt. 4:21). He, along with James and Peter, had a special relationship with the Lord (Mark 5:37; 13:3). John is mentioned only three times in the book of Acts (3:1; 4:13; 8:14), and tradition says that he settled in Ephesus, where he was later arrested and banished under the Emperor Domitian to Patmos (a small island in the Aegean Sea) to work in the mines.[1] Domitian reigned from AD 81–96, and since

Irenaeus's testimony that John wrote Revelation while on Patmos is confirmed by other early writers, the book is apparently one of the last written of the New Testament. This late date (in the 90s) is also confirmed by the picture of complacency and defection in the churches in chapters 2 and 3. This fact presupposes that a second generation of Christians had already come on the scene who did not hold the same convictions as their fathers. That the style of Revelation is different from the Gospel and the three letters of John is no proof that Revelation was written by a different John. The nature of the material in Revelation and the fact that it was given in a vision can easily account for the differences in style.

INTERPRETATIONS OF THE BOOK

The book is a revelation of things that must soon take place. The understanding of when the events of the book come to pass marks the difference between the various schools of interpretation.

Preterist

"Preterist" is from a Latin word that means "past." Thus the preterist interpreters are those who see Revelation as having already been fulfilled in the early centuries of the church. Chapters 5–11 are said to record the church's victory over Judaism; chapters 12–19, her victory over pagan Rome; and chapters 20–22, her glory because of these victories. The persecutions described are those of Nero and Domitian, and the entire book was fulfilled by the time of Constantine (AD 312).

Historical or Continuous-Historical

The historical or continuous-historical interpretive viewpoint states that in Revelation there is a panorama of the history of the church from the days of John to the end of the age. It holds that the book has been in the process of being fulfilled throughout the whole Christian era. Those who hold to this view see in the symbols the rise of the papacy, the corruption of the church, and various wars throughout church history. Most of the Reformers interpreted the book in this manner, but everyone's interpretation within this viewpoint is a scheme all its own. There is no uniformity of details; indeed, dogmatism and contradiction abound among those who attempt to interpret the book in this way.

Idealist

The idealist approach sees in Revelation a pictorial unfolding of great principles in constant conflict. The book does not record actual events that have been fulfilled or that are going to happen; rather, it merely portrays the age-long struggle between good and evil. This viewpoint spiritualizes and allegorizes the text.

Futurist or Normal Interpretation

The label "futurist" is derived from the fact that this interpretation sees the book from chapter 4 to the end as yet to be fulfilled. If one follows the plain, literal, or normal principle of interpretation, one concludes that most of the book describes what is yet future. No judgments in history have ever equaled those described in chapters 6, 8, 9, and 16. The resurrections and judgment described in chapter 20 have not yet occurred. There has been no visible return of Christ as portrayed in chapter 19.

The concept of a literal interpretation raises questions for some, since it seems to preclude anything symbolic, and the book obviously contains symbols. Perhaps saying "normal" or "plain" would be better than "literal," since futurists do recognize the use of symbols in the book. The difference between the literalist and the spiritualizer is simply that the former sees the symbols as conveying a plain meaning. All recognize the presence of symbols in the Bible. Note, for instance, Psalm 22. Verse 18 prophesied the casting of lots for Christ's garments. This was a literal statement. Verses 12 and 13 depict the fierce enemies of the Lord as strong bulls and ravening lions. These are symbols with a very plain meaning.

Revelation 8:12 prophesies a judgment that will affect the sun, moon, stars, day, and night. Apparently the stars are the literal astronomical bodies in the heavens. In 9:1–2 John records seeing a star fall from heaven. This is a plain symbol, and one that is interpreted in the text itself as indicating a created being (probably an angel). The English word "star" is used today in both a literal and symbolic manner, just as it is in Revelation 8 and 9. We speak literally of the stars in the heavens. We also refer to stars on the athletic field or in the entertainment industry, and in so doing we are using a symbol with a very plain meaning. Indeed, symbols often make the meaning *more* plain.

Futurists do not deny the presence of symbols in the book, nor do they claim to be able to explain every detail with certainty. But they do insist that the principle of plain interpretation be followed consistently throughout the book.

In interpreting this book it is also important to remember that John often was shown things he struggled to describe in earthly language. Therefore, he says something is "like" something else (as, e.g., in his description of the risen Christ in 1:13–16 and the appearances of the locusts in 9:7–10). Or he will use "as" to try to best convey what he saw or heard (e.g., 6:12–13). Both words are used together in 13:11. But when he does not use these words, we are to understand that whatever he is describing is exactly what he saw or heard.

ATTITUDES TOWARD THE BOOK

Generally speaking, there are two attitudes toward Revelation. Some say the book cannot be understood and therefore should not be studied, taught, or preached. Differences of interpretation, they point out, have divided Christians; therefore, one should not attempt to interpret the book. Of course, most biblical doctrines have been differently interpreted and in some cases have caused divisions in the church. But that certainly does not mean we should not seek to understand those doctrines and interpret them correctly. Others consider themselves so sure of every detail in the book that they set dates and propose highly fanciful interpretations. To them, Revelation seems to be the only book in the Bible worth studying.

The proper attitude toward this book does not lie in either extreme. The book is important and profitable, as is all Scripture (2 Tim. 3:16), but it is not the only book in the Bible worthy of close scrutiny. Let us approach it as worthy of all the Spirit-directed and careful study we can give it, focusing every God-given ability on its words and fitting it into the whole of God's truth as contained in the Bible. Let our approach never be theoretical and detached, but always personal and involved.

Even though this book is largely about the future, knowledge of it should affect our living in the present. James encouraged his contemporaries with the knowledge of future judgment (James 5:8), and Paul wrote of the assurance that comes from knowing that Satan will eventually be defeated (Rom. 16:20). God can motivate believers today by the understanding of those things He has revealed through John in Revelation.

OUTLINE OF THE BOOK

Prologue (1:1–8)

  I. "The things which you have seen" (1:9–20)

 II. "The things which are" (2:1–3:22)

III. "The things which shall take place after these things"
(4:1–22:21)

    Prologue (4:1–5:14)

    A. The Tribulation (6:1–19:21)

    B. The Millennium (20:1–15)

    C. The Eternal State (21:1–22:5)

    Epilogue (22:6–21)

AN OVERVIEW OF REVELATION

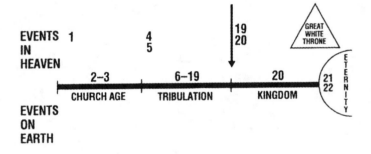

THE PROLOGUE

1:1–8

....

THE SUPERSCRIPTION, 1:1–3

The Title, 1:1

Although it is true that this book reveals Christ, the genitive expression "of Jesus Christ" means that it is a revelation given *by* Christ. It is a revelation of "things which must soon take place." The words translated "soon" (*en tachei*) mean that when the time for judgment comes there will be no delay in its execution (see Luke 18:8 and other occurrences of this phrase in Acts 12:7; 22:18; 25:4; Rom. 16:20; Rev. 22:6–7). The time of the fulfillment may seem distant, but, when it starts, the events will transpire rapidly.

The Means of Communication, 1:1–2

The chain of communication was God the Father, to Christ, to an angel, to John, to God's servants. John, the human instrument, testified of the Word of God (he considered himself in the prophetic succession, transmitting God's message to humanity) and the testimony of Christ (that is, the witness Christ imparts about Himself).

The Value of The Book, 1:3

A blessing is promised the person reading and those hearing and keeping the words of the book. Note the change from singular to plural—one reads and several hear—indicating that the book was to be read publicly. Since public reading was one test of canonicity, the fact that John indicates that it should be read publicly means that he considered it canonical. The entire book is called a prophecy. The phrase "the time is near" is repeated in the epilogue (22:10). "Near" *(engus)* means "impending or at hand"; these events are near because a thousand years are as a day with the Lord (2 Peter 3:8).

THE SALUTATION, 1:4–8

The Writer, 1:4

The Hebrew idioms in the book, the authority of the author in relation to the churches, the use of distinctively Johannine terms such as *logos* and "Lamb of God," and the corroboration of Irenaeus, Origen, Tertullian, and Clement all affirm that the apostle John was the author of this book.

The Readers, 1:4

The fact that John specifically addressed the seven local churches in Asia Minor prevents anyone from saying that the book is simply a piece of poetic idealism.

The Greeting, 1:4–5a

This is a greeting from the Trinity. The Father eternally existed and will always exist (the phrase "who is and who was and who is to come" occurs also in 1:8; 4:8; 11:17; 16:5). The "seven Spirits" likely represent the sevenfold ministry of the Spirit as depicted in Isaiah 11:2. Christ is designated as (1) the faithful Witness (summarizing His life on earth, cf. John 7:7; 8:18; 1 Tim. 6:13),

(2) the Firstborn from the dead (His resurrection), and (3) the Ruler (not "prince") of the kings of the earth, which refers to His future reign over the earth.

The Dedication, 1:5b–6

The book is dedicated to Christ, who was its Author and about whom it speaks. Three things are ascribed to Him: (1) He loves (present tense) us. (2) He released us (some translations say "washed," the difference in Greek being one letter) from our sins by His blood. Blood is the evidence of His death, which is the basis for our cleansing. (3) He made us a kingdom (not "kings") and priests to God. "Kingdom" views believers corporately and anticipates our association with Christ in His future reign (5:9–10), whereas "priests" sees them individually ministering to our Lord forever.

The Keynote, 1:7

Verse 7 is the text, theme, or keynote of the book and is a reference to Christ's second coming. It is after the Tribulation (note Matt. 24:29–30), it will be public, and all shall see Him and bemoan His crucifixion. This is partly quoted from Zechariah 12:10. "Tribes" is not limited to Israel but includes all the peoples of the earth.

The Authentication, 1:8

Some understand the speaker in verse 8 to be God; others, Christ. It is probably God verifying the contents of this prophecy. Alpha and Omega are the first and last letters of the Greek alphabet, signifying the completeness of God. He is the Lord God, eternally existing, and all-powerful. "Almighty" is used eight times in Revelation (1:8; 4:8; 11:17; 15:3; 16:7, 14; 19:6; 21:22) and includes the ideas of omnipotence and universal rulership.

OUTLINE OF REVELATION

I "The things which you have seen" (chapter 1)

- The Risen Christ

II "The things which are" (chapters 2–3)

- The Letters to the Seven Churches

   Ephesus · Smyrna · Pergamum · Thyatira
   Sardis · Philadelphia · Laodicea

III "The things which shall take place after these things"

- The Tribulation (chapters 4–19)

   CHAPTER

4. The Throne in Heaven	13. Antichrist & False Prophet
5. The Scroll in Heaven	14. Announcements
6. SEALS	15. Prelude to Bowls
7. The Redeemed	16. BOWLS
8-9. TRUMPETS	17. Religious Babylon
10. The Little Scroll	18. Commercial Babylon
11. The Two Witnesses	19. Second Coming of Christ

- The Millennium (chapter 20)

- The Eternal State (chapters 21–22)

THE VISION OF THE RISEN CHRIST

1:9–20

....

Although there is more than one way to divide the book of Revelation, most commentators see in 1:19 the divinely given outline. In this verse the book is divided into three parts: (1) the things John had seen up to verse 19, (2) the present state of the church (chaps. 2–3), and (3) the things that shall be after the church is completed (chaps. 4–22). The same words translated "after these things" *(meta tauta)* are found in 4:1, indicating that chapter 4 begins this last section of the book. However, it is possible to combine the first two sections because verse 19 may well be translated, "Write the things which you have seen, and the things which are, and..."

In other words, John saw two things: present things and future things. The present things include the vision of Christ in 1:9–20 and the letters to the churches in chapters 2 and 3. Of course, it does make sense to see 1:9–3:22 as one unified section, simply because in the vision in 1:9–20 Christ is walking in the midst of those churches mentioned in chapters 2 and 3. But it is equally valid to consider the vision of 1:9–20 as that which John had seen and thus as a separate division of the book. The important thing is to notice that according to 1:19 the book has to divide at 4:1, regardless of whether one combines the vision of 1:9–20 with chapters 2 and 3 or divides it into a separate section. Understanding that 4:1 begins the section that describes the future after the times of the churches ends supports a pretribulation Rapture view. In other words, the period of the churches ends at 3:22, and the events of the Tribulation begin to be described at 4:1— "things which must take place [the future Tribulation, return of Christ, and the Millennium] after these things [the completion of the church age]." Posttribulationists who believe that the church will live through the Tribulation on this earth understand 4:1 to indicate only the time when John saw the vision, that is, after he received the letters to the seven churches. But since "after these things" is similar to the phrase in Daniel 2:29, "what will take place," where it clearly refers to the content of Nebuchadnezzar's dream, which concerned the future, then it should be understood in John's use as also referring to the eschatological future.

SECTION 1:

"THE THINGS WHICH YOU HAVE SEEN," 1:9–20

Circumstances of the Vision, 1:9–11

John's Physical Circumstances, 1:9

John does not exalt himself above his fellow believers but calls himself a brother. Patmos is an island about fifteen miles in circumference in the Aegean Sea southwest of Ephesus. The reason for his banishment was because of "the word of God" (God's claims on men) and "the testimony of Jesus" (the gospel message).

John's Spiritual Circumstances, 1:10–11

John's being in the Spirit seems to indicate a trancelike state of spiritual ecstasy. "Was" is literally "became," indicating that this was something unusual. The phrase "the Lord's day" could refer to Sunday or the Day of the Lord, that is, the Tribulation and the Millennium, which are the subject of much of the prophecy. "Lord's" is an adjective (*kyriakos*), used only here and in 1 Corinthians 11:20 in the New Testament. Outside the New Testament it means "imperial." Unless this is a reference to Sunday, there is no place in the New Testament where this expression is used for that day, since the usual designation is "first day of the week." It could, therefore, refer to that imperial day in the future when Christ will take the reins of earthly government, which is what John saw in his vision. The voice John heard was that of Christ, who is identified as the First and Last in verse 17. All that John saw (cf. 22:8), not just the particular letter to each church in chapters 2–3, was to be communicated to all these seven churches mentioned in verse 11.

The Content of the Vision, 1:12–16

The Position of the Lord, 1:12–13

We have very little knowledge of what our Lord looked like while He was here on earth. He apparently had a beard (Isa. 50:6). There was nothing in His overall personal appearance that would especially attract people to Him (Isa. 53:2), though children liked Him (Matt. 18:2). In this section, however, is a description of how He appears in glory and how we shall see Him some day, for, as John wrote elsewhere, "we will see Him just as He is," not as He *was* (1 John 3:2).

The Picture of the Lord, 1:14–16

This picture of the risen, glorified Lord is depicted under a number of similes (note the occurrences of "like" and "as")—the only way He could be described to finite creatures. There are seven features to this picture, and the meaning of these similes may have been left unexplained deliberately in order to convey more than one thing to our minds.

His head, 1:14. It was white as wool or snow. This may represent the wisdom of age and the purity of holiness (Prov. 20:29).

His eyes, 1:14. They were piercing in their fiery holiness. The true character of each church is transparent to His eyes. There may also be a connection between this verse and 1 Corinthians 3:13; that is, the fire that shall try human works at the judgment seat of Christ will be the penetrating gaze of our Lord, which will of itself consume works of wood, hay, and straw.

His feet, 1:15. John's eyes dropped from the Lord's eyes to His feet, which were like burnished bronze. ("Burnished" means "highly rubbed and polished.") This may picture the trials He experienced in His earthly life that make Him a sympathetic High Priest (Heb. 4:15) and an experienced Judge.

His voice, 1:15. It was to John as the sound of many waters. Like the noise of a mighty waterfall, His voice of authority stands out above all the rest and drowns out all who try to talk back or offer excuses to Him.

His right hand, 1:16. In His right hand, the place of honor, were the seven stars, which are explained in verse 20 as the messengers of the churches of chapters 2–3. The word *angelos* ("angel") means "messenger" and could refer to a supernatural being, implying that each church has its guardian angel. The word could also be used in the nontechnical sense of a human messenger (see James 2:25 and Luke 9:52)—the human leader or pastor of the church.

His mouth, 1:16. The Word of God, the basis for all judgment, proceeded out of His mouth (Heb. 4:12; Rev. 19:12–15).

His countenance, 1:16. Christ's overall appearance was such that it overwhelmed John.

Consequences of the Vision, 1:17–20
A Word of Comfort 1:17–18

The awesomeness of the vision caused John to prostrate himself before the glorified Christ, waiting for His mercy. This resulted in a threefold word of comfort for the aged apostle. Christ presented Himself as the self-existent, eternal One, "the first and the last"; the Conqueror over death; and the One who controls (by having the keys) Hades (the place that holds the immaterial part of humans after physical death) and death (the experience of the material part).

A Word of Command, 1:19–20

The apostle is then commanded to write the things that he had seen and would yet see. As stated, this forms an outline of the book and is followed in verse 20 by the Lord's own explanation of two features of the vision. The "stars" are the angels (either guardian angels or the human leaders) of the churches, and the "lampstands" represent light-bearing local churches.

THE SEVEN CHURCHES OF ASIA

THE CHURCHES OF REVELATION 2–3

DESTINATION	THE LORD	COMMENDATION	CONDEMNATION	EXHORTATIONS	PROMISE 1 John 5:4-5
EPHESUS 2:1-7 • FREE CITY Acts 19:35 • TEMPLE OF DIANA • COMMERCIAL CENTER	• HOLDING 7 STARS • WALKING AMONG CHURCHES	• WORKS • ENDURANCE • DISCERNMENT • HATRED OF NICOLAITANS	• LEFT FIRST LOVE	• REMEMBER • REPENT • REPEAT FIRST WORKS	• ETERNAL (TREE OF) LIFE
SMYRNA 2:8-11 • TRADE CENTER • BEAUTIFUL CITY • FREE CITY • CENTER OF CAESAR WORSHIP • JEWISH POPULATION	• GUARANTOR OF RESURRECTION	• SPIRITUAL WEALTH	• NONE	• DO NOT FEAR • DO BE FAITHFUL	• RESURRECTION TO LIFE (NO PART IN SECOND DEATH)
PERGAMUM 2:12-17 • 200,000 VOLUME LIBRARY • WORSHIP OF ASKLEPIOS • CENTER OF CAESAR WORSHIP	• JUDGE (SWORD)	• STEADFASTNESS	• IDOLATRY • IMMORALITY • LICENSE	• REPENT	• CHRIST IS SUFFICIENT

DESTINATION	THE LORD	COMMENDATION	CONDEMNATION	EXHORTATIONS	PROMISE 1 John 5:4-5
THYATIRA 2:18-29 • TRADE CENTER ACTS 16:14 • GUILDS	• JUDGE (EYES, FEET)	• INCREASING NUMBER OF GOOD WORKS	• FOLLOWING JEZEBEL'S TEACHINGS AND PRACTICES	• KEEP FROM JEZEBEL'S SINS	• SHARING CHRIST'S RULE AND FELLOWSHIP
SARDIS 3:1-6 • TRADE CENTER, DYEING • WORSHIP OF CYBELE • LOOSE LIVING	• WISE AND SOVEREIGN ONE	• ONLY A FEW WERE FAITHFUL	• LIFELESS PROFESSION • INCOMPLETE WORKS	• REMEMBER • REPENT • WATCH	• ASSURANCE OF ETERNAL LIFE
PHILADELPHIA 3:7-13 • GRAPE GROWING • WORSHIP OF DIONYSIUS • EARTHQUAKES	• HOLY, TRUE, SOVEREIGN	• USING OPPORTUNITIES • A LITTLE POWER • KEEPING HIS WORD • FIDELITY	• NONE	• HOLD FAST	• HUMILIATION OF ENEMIES • DELIVERANCE • I COME QUICKLY • HONOR • IDENTIFICATION
LAODICEA 3:14-22 • BANKING CENTER • BLACK WOOL • MEDICINES	• FAITHFUL AND TRUE	• NONE	• SPIRITUAL PROFESSION • SPIRITUAL POVERTY	• FIND TRUE RICHES IN CHRIST	• CONTINUING AND BOUNTIFUL FELLOWSHIP WITH CHRIST

THE
SEVEN CHURCHES

2:1–3:22

....

The seven churches addressed by letter in chapters 2 and 3 are significant in several ways. First of all, at the time John wrote they were actual churches that existed in the cities mentioned. They were not necessarily the most prominent ones of that day, since only two—Ephesus and Laodicea—are previously mentioned in the Bible. But they were actual churches with problems and strengths recorded of them. This means, of course, that, just as there was an Ephesian church in John's day, there was also a Laodicean church in the first century.

These churches were representative of all churches at that time, as well as those of subsequent generations. Just as the letters to the Corinthians, though written to the church at Corinth, concern the church everywhere and at all times (1 Cor. 1:2), so these letters are for the church past, present, and future.

Two reasons substantiate the representative character of these seven churches. The first is simply that there are only seven selected. Out of all the churches that might have been chosen (though not all in Asia Minor), such as Jerusalem, Antioch, Alexandria,

Corinth, Rome, Troas, Colossae, or Hierapolis, only seven are selected. Second, in the promise to each of these churches at the close of each letter is the exhortation to hear what the Spirit says to "the churches." Though each letter is written to *a* church, the exhortations are to *all* the churches.

Some see a third significance of these churches, regarding them as representing seven successive periods throughout church history. One writer says, "The varying conditions represented in these seven churches in order of their succession fit uniquely into the checkered history of the church universal from start to finish."[1] This idea does not deny their local and representative character, but it often tends to obscure their local and representative importance by placing so much emphasis on the Philadelphian or Laodicean church as the era in which the church is presently living. We forget that there are many local churches today with, for example, Ephesian and Pergamum characteristics.

Each letter is addressed to the angel of the particular church. The word "angel," as previously discussed, can refer to either a superhuman or human being. If *angel* refers to the human leader of each church, then that leader's responsibility for the condition of the church is emphasized in the address of each letter: "to the angel of the church . . ."

SECTION 2:
"THE THINGS WHICH ARE," 2:1–3:22

These letters comprise the "things which are." They depict conditions that did and do exist in the churches, then and now. Each letter may be outlined under six headings: Destination, The Lord, Commendation, Condemnation, Exhortations, and Promise.

The Letter to Ephesus, 2:1–7

Destination, 2:1

Ephesus was the capital of the province of Asia and the residence of John before and after his exile on Patmos. A city of about 300,000, it was a commercial center with warehouses that lined the banks of the Cayster River. It was on a principal east-west road. Pan-Ionian games were held there in May. It was known throughout the world as the home of one of the seven wonders of the ancient world—the temple of Diana. This magnificent structure stood in an area 425 by 220 feet, with 126 pillars of marble 60 feet high. Thirty-six of these were overlaid with gold and jewels. Eunuchs and slaves attended the temple, and the city proudly entitled itself the guardian of the temple and statue of Diana (Acts 19:35).

At the close of his second missionary trip, Paul visited the city briefly (Acts 18:18–19) but returned for over two years on his third trip to found and establish the church there (Acts 19). During that time, through the efforts of ordinary believers, all the province of Asia "heard the word of the Lord" (Acts 19:10), and there were more than five hundred urban communities in the province! There, too, a great number of believers dedicated themselves more fully to the Lord after they burned their books of magic, which some had evidently been hanging on to for two or more years. The value of the books was equivalent to a year's wage for 138 workers. The church counted Aquila, Priscilla, Apollos, Timothy, and John among its spiritual leaders. Ephesus (meaning "desirable") may represent the apostolic age.

The Lord, 2:1

In each letter the risen Christ presented Himself in a particular fashion, usually selected from the representation in chapter 1, that was especially relevant to the conditions of the church addressed. In this instance (in view of the loss of first love), the Lord's watchful relationship to local churches and their leaders is emphasized in two ways: He is seen holding fast (*krateo*) the seven stars or angels (in contrast to 1:16, where He merely has them), and He is walking (in contrast to standing, 1:13) in the midst of the churches.

Commendation, 2:2–3, 6

The church is commended for her works, perseverance, discernment in testing, rejection of false apostles, and hatred of the Nicolaitans. Some understand the Nicolaitan error to be the exaltation of the clergy over the laity (based on the etymology of the word itself, which means "laity-conqueror"). Others consider it to be the heresy of license and compromise in matters of Christian conduct, since it is associated in 2:14–15 with the doctrine of Balaam, who tried to induce God's people to compromise.

Condemnation, 2:4

The church has "left" (not "lost") her first love. This was a deliberate and thus responsible action, for the word means "to quit or forsake." The original spiritual vitality of the church had been replaced by a routine of orthodoxy. Paul may have sounded a warning that this would happen when years before he pronounced his benediction on Ephesian Christians who loved the Lord with an incorruptible, or pure, love (Eph. 6:24). First love, then, is love without any impurities.

Exhortation, 2:5–6

The exhortation was to remember, repent, and repeat her first works of love. Notice that they were to do their first *works,* not to feel their first *feelings.*

Promise, 2:7

An overcomer is not one who has some special power in the Christian life or who has learned some secret of victory. John himself defined an overcomer as a believer in Christ (1 John 5:4–5). Thus every Christian is an overcomer, though the various promises in these seven letters are addressed particularly to each local believing group and tailored to the special circumstances found in each church. Believers here are promised the tree of life, that is, eternal life, which was lost when Adam sinned in the garden (Gen. 2:9; 3:22; Rev. 22:2, 14). And, of course, all believers possess eternal life forever.

The Letter to Smyrna, 2:8–11

Destination, 2:8

Smyrna (Izmir today}, about thirty-five miles north of Ephesus, was and continues to be an important seaport city. It also was a commercial center known for its trade in wines. It was a beautiful city and the site of many temples, including one erected in honor of the Emperor Tiberias. It boasted a stadium and a library. There were many apostate Jews there who were often leaders in agitating persecution of Christians. The word itself means "bitter," being translated elsewhere in the New Testament as "myrrh" (Matt. 2:11; Mark 15:23; John 19:39). If it represents an era in church history, it pictures the postapostolic era up to the time when Constantine espoused the Christian faith.

It was also a center of growing worship of Caesar. This evolved from "a spirit of Rome" to "gratitude for Rome" to "the peace of Rome" and finally to "the god of Rome" embodied in the emperor. In other words, a man-god was being substituted for the God-man. In its early stages emperor worship was voluntary, but patriotic/religious enthusiasm began to make it compulsory. A pinch of incense was offered to Caesar to show the worshiper's devotion and allegiance to Caesar. For this act the worshiper received a certificate. One such read, "We, the representatives of the Emperor, Severos and Hermas, have seen you sacrificing." Even though one acknowledged Caesar as Lord, he or she could also worship other gods as well, but a Christian could do neither.

The Lord, 2:8

To a church under persecution, many of whose members would experience martyrdom, the Lord appropriately presents Himself as the One who died and lived, thus assuring them of the hope of resurrection.

Commendation, 2:9

The church is commended for its wealth in the midst of the most trying circumstances. Of course, this is spiritual wealth, for they were poor and persecuted. The instigators of the persecution were apostate Jews who were in reality instruments of Satan. When Polycarp was martyred at Smyrna in AD 155, these Jews eagerly assisted by gathering *on the Sabbath* wood and fagots for the fire in which he was burned.

Exhortation, 2:10

In place of any word of condemnation (as also in the case of the church at Philadelphia), there is exhortation not to fear and a promise of a crown of life for faithfulness (cf. James 1:12). Satan would move people to cast some of these believers into prison, and persecution for "ten days" would result in some being killed. The ten days may refer to a brief, intense time of trouble, or it may indicate the ten principal persecutions under the Roman emperors from Nero to Diocletian.

Promise, 2:11

The promise to the believer-overcomer is that he or she shall not have a part in the second death, which is the Lake of Fire (20:14; 21:8). In other words, the believer will share in the resurrection, not in the torment that awaits the unbeliever. The certainty of this promise is emphasized by the use of a double negative in the text.

The Letter to Pergamum, 2:12–17

Destination, 2:12

The two parts of the name "Pergamum" (about forty-five miles north of Smyrna and seventy-five miles north of Ephesus) mean "elevation and marriage." For many centuries it was an independent kingdom, but it became part of the Roman Empire in 133 BC and the location of the only provincial temple of the imperial cult in Asia erected in honor of Augustus Caesar (who reigned when Jesus was born). It also boasted one of the finest libraries of antiquity, with two hundred thousand books (all manuscripts), and was the place where skins were first used for writing on. Papyrus, which disintegrates over a relatively short period of time, was replaced by long-lasting skins. This is evidence of the providence of God, for otherwise we would have far fewer copies of ancient manuscripts of the New Testament. This church might characterize the period beginning with the legalizing of Christianity by Constantine in AD 313.

The Lord, 2:12 (cf. 1:16)

The two-edged sword is the symbol of the word of Christ, the assurance of judgment on the basis of absolute truth.

Commendation, 2:13

The Lord commends the church for its steadfastness in the very center of Satan's domination. Antipas (either one of their members or someone brought to Pergamum for trial) had already suffered martyrdom. "Satan's throne" refers to pagan Pergamum's worship either of the Roman emperor (for like Smyrna it was a center of emperor worship) or of the Greek gods in the temple or of Zeus at his altar on the Acropolis (or all three). Among the gods worshiped were Dionysus, the god of wine, and Asklepios, the god of healing. Snakes were associated with the worship of both gods. Little wonder the city was the throne of Satan, the serpent.

Condemnation, 2:14–15

The condemnation was in the realm of morals (doctrine of Balaam) and of doctrine (the Nicolaitans). Balaam (Num. 22:1–24:25), finding himself unable to curse God's people, instructed Balak king of Moab to corrupt them through immorality and idolatry so that God eventually judged them. His doctrine is the teaching of compromise in life. As noted earlier, the doctrine of the Nicolaitans may be the same teaching (i.e., compromise) or it may be an unwarranted exaltation of the clergy. Meals consisting of meats sacrificed to idols were generally held in heathen temples, and the believers are forbidden to participate (cf. 1 Cor. 10:14–22).

Exhortation, 2:16

The call to repentance is coupled with a warning of judgment on the basis of the Word of God.

Promise, 2:17

Hidden manna is the sufficiency of Christ in contrast to the allurements of the world that compromise offered. Manna replaces meats offered to idols. The meaning of the white stone with the new name written is derived from either or both of two customs of the day. The first was that of judges, who determined a verdict by placing in an urn a white and a black pebble. If the white one came out, it meant acquittal; thus the white stone would mean the assurance that there is no condemnation to those who are in Christ Jesus. The other custom was the wearing of amulets as good luck charms around the neck. If this is the reference, then the stone is the Lord's way of reminding the people that they had Him and needed no other thing.

The Letter to Thyatira, 2:18–29

Destination, 2:18

Thyatira, about thirty-five miles southeast of Pergamum, was noted for its numerous trade guilds and for its wool and dyeing industry. It was the home of Lydia, who traded in cloth that was dyed purple (Acts 16:14). The name means "unweary sacrifice," and if these churches picture eras of church history, Thyatira—both because of its name and the activity of Jezebel—depicts the Middle Ages and the ascendancy of the Roman Catholic Church.

The Lord, 2:18

The Lord represents Himself to the church as the divine one ("Son of God") who is the executor of searching judgment ("eyes like a flame of fire"), trampling His enemies under His feet (v. 27).

Commendation, 2:19

The church is commended for increasing in good works.

Condemnation, 2:20–23

The church is rebuked for permitting the false teaching of a prophetess who openly advocated apostasy. Her actual name may or may not have been Jezebel, but she was a true Jezebel in her actions (1 Kings 19; 2 Kings 9). She promoted immorality and idolatry (v. 20) in a doctrinal context that is described as the "deep things of Satan"—his attempt to make wrong seem right (v. 24). Because she had not repented in spite of the patience of God, He promised to judge her by allowing her a complete abandonment to her way of life (v. 22), trouble for her followers ("her children," v. 23), and eventual death, all of which was calculated to wake up the church (v. 23).

Exhortation, 2:24–25

The exhortation to those who had not trafficked with Jezebel was "no other burden" than that they should themselves keep from immorality and idolatry. The phrase is an echo of Acts 15:28–29.

Promise, 2:26–28

The faithful are promised association with Christ in His millennial reign (vv. 26–27; cf. Ps. 2:9) and "the morning star" (v. 28). This is a reference to Christ Himself (cf. 22:16) and/or to the immortal life we receive from Him.

The Letter to Sardis, 3:1–6
Destination, 3:1

Sardis, about thirty miles south of Thyatira, was the capital of Lydia. The city was thought to be impregnable, but Cyrus, king of the Medo-Persians, captured it by following a secret path up the cliff. The word "Sardis" is probably from a Hebrew word meaning "rest" or "remnant." The city was a trading center for wool and dyeing and was characterized by a loose, luxurious lifestyle. The church was at peace—the peace of the dead! This church may represent the Reformation period in church history.

The Lord, 3:1

The Lord appears as the One who is full of wisdom ("seven Spirits") and who is in complete control of the leadership of the churches ("seven stars," cf. 1:20).

Commendation, 3:4

The relatively few faithful saints are commended, though the church in general was dead.

Condemnation, 3:1–2

The church is first condemned for its lifeless profession (v. 1). The One who knows all things discerned the true condition of the church as being dead, though outwardly it seemed alive. Second, the church is condemned for its incomplete works (v. 2).

Exhortation, 3:3

Like the church at Ephesus, this one is exhorted to remember what they had received and heard in the first days of their Christian experience (cf. Heb. 10:32; Gal. 5:7). The people are also exhorted to watch for the Lord's coming and to be prepared (1 Thess. 5:6–8).

Promise, 3:5–6

To the true believing remnant in the church is promised white raiment, a sign of purity (cf. 19:8, 14). The grace of the Lord is displayed in the statement of verse 4 that these few are worthy to walk with the Lord in purity. The certainty of the promise is assured because these will *not* (emphatic double negative) be blotted out of the Book of Life (cf. 20:12). This statement does not threaten the possible loss of one's salvation but rather promises assurance that no believer will ever lose it. Also, these faithful ones will be acknowledged publicly before the Father and His angels.

The Letter to Philadelphia, 3:7–13

Destination, 3:7

Philadelphia, about twenty-eight miles southeast of Sardis, means "brotherly love." The city was named after King Attalus III. It bordered on Mysia, Lydia, and Phrygia, and, because it was liable to severe earthquakes, many of its inhabitants lived outside the city limits. Though many gods were worshiped there, its principal deity was Dionysus, the god of wine. This church displays characteristics of the modern missionary era of church history.

The Lord, 3:7

The Head of the church presents Himself as holy, true, and authoritative. The last part of verse 7 is taken from Isaiah 22:22, where authority was given God's servant Eliakim over David's house, just as Christ has authority over His church.

Commendation, 3:8

The church is commended for four things: (1) using the opportunities afforded by the open door (this seems to be implied in v. 8); (2) a little power (not so much an indication of spiritual weakness as of the few true saints in the church); (3) keeping His Word; and (4) separation from evil and faithfulness to Him.

Promises, 3:9–11, 12–13

Four promises are given.

Enemies will be humiliated. Their enemies will be humiliated before them (v. 9). As in Smyrna, these unbelieving Jewish antagonists are called the "synagogue of Satan"(2:9).

The church will be delivered from the Tribulation. The church is also promised deliverance from the hour of trial that shall come upon all the world. The words "temptation" or "trial" are equivalents for "tribulation" (cf. Luke 8:13 with Matt. 13:21 and Mark 4:17). The verse indicates that this does not refer to the normal trials of Christians (John 16:33; Acts 14:22), but to a special "hour of testing," which will be worldwide. Even the persecutions that believers have and are suffering today at the hands of particular nations do not fulfill this verse, since they are not worldwide. The promise of the Lord is that the church will be kept from that hour by being raptured to heaven.

This is the pretribulation view of the relation of the Rapture to the Tribulation; that is, the church will be raptured before (pre-) the Tribulation begins. Another view teaches that the church will live through the first half of the Tribulation and be raptured at the midpoint (mid-tribulationism). This view supposes that the first half will be a time of peace and that the terrible judgments will not begin until the midpoint. A third view says that the church will live through the entire period of tribulation, being protected by God, and will be raptured at the end. In this view, the Rapture is still a distinct event that occurs just at the end of the Tribulation and is immediately followed by the return of Christ to earth.

It is well known that the phrase "keep . . . from" is used only twice in the New Testament—here and in John 17:15. Post-tribulationists say that comparing John 17:15 with Revelation 3:10 shows us that just as believers in the world are kept from Satan's power now, so will those living in the Tribulation be kept from its judgments. However, the Lord's prayer that believers be kept from the evil one is answered by delivering us from the power of darkness and transferring us into the kingdom of His beloved Son (Col. 1:13). By this transfer we have been removed from the kingdom of darkness. Similarly Revelation 3:10 promises us removal from the time of the worldwide Tribulation by being taken to heaven in the Rapture of the church before that time begins. This is not a promise of protection while living through the Tribulation on earth but removal and transfer from earth to heaven (just as we have been transferred into His kingdom). In this passage, believers of the Church Age are promised they will be kept from that hour not by being protected while living on earth during that awful time, but by being taken to heaven in the Rapture of the church before that time begins.

Although the most natural meaning of Revelation 3:10 sees it as a promise to transfer us from the earth, where the hour of trial will be going on, it is at least theoretically possible to conceive of the church's being protected from the judgments of the tribulation period while remaining on earth. However, we know that God's saints on the earth during that time will not be exempt from the judgments or from death (6:9–11; 7:9–14; 14:1–3; 15:1–3). Many church saints will suffer and die along with Tribulation believers if the church goes through the Tribulation. Furthermore, people might be preserved in the Tribulation without a pretribulation Rapture, but how can they be kept from the hour, or time, of the Tribulation without being removed from the earth, the place where the events of that time are happening? If the church will not be raptured before the hour begins, then the promise will not be fulfilled, because many saints simply will not be preserved in the Tribulation but will suffer and die along with unsaved people.

Believers will be honored. The promise that believers will be pillars may allude to the custom in Philadelphia of honoring a magistrate or philanthropist by placing a great pillar with his name inscribed on it in one of the temples. Believers will be so honored in the temple of God and permanently so ("will not go out from it any more," v. 12).

Saints will have God's name. God promises to write on the saints His name, the name of His city, and Christ's new name.

TRIBULATION VIEWS

PRETRIBULATIONISM

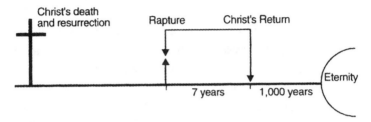

MIDTRIBULATIONISM

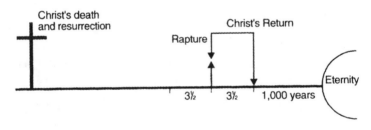

POSTTRIBULATIONISM

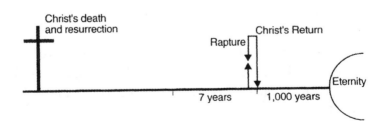

What the new name may be we do not know, but the writing of this name indicates identification with, and possession by, God.

These must have been very precious promises to a church that was plagued by enemies within and without, and they will always be precious promises to the church universal in every age.

Exhortation, 3:11

The only exhortation is to "hold fast" (the same word used in 2:1, 13–14, 25). The reason for this exhortation is so that no one would rob them of their rewards (cf. 2 John 8).

The Letter to Laodicea, 3:14–22

Destination, 3:14

These seven churches lie within a great geographic arc beginning with Ephesus, swinging northward through Smyrna and Pergamum, and southeast to Laodicea. This last city is about ninety miles due east of Ephesus and about forty-five miles southeast of Philadelphia. It was a wealthy city, able to rebuild itself in AD 60 without the aid of Rome (or God!). It was also a medical center known for an ointment for treating ears and a powder for the eyes. The church, like the city, put its trust in material things rather than spiritual. The name of the town means "judgment of the people," and the church exhibits characteristics of the modern period.

The Lord, 3:14

The risen Lord presents Himself to this church as "the Amen" (confirming all that He says), "the faithful and true Witness" in contrast to all the false prophets, and "the Beginning of the creation of God" (indicating His priority over all creation; cf. Col. 1:17). He is the unalterable standard by which all must be measured.

Condemnation, 3:15–17

Though outwardly this church must have appeared strong and prosperous, the Lord finds nothing to commend. His stern condemnation is against two things:

1. Gross indifference (vv. 15–16). Near Laodicea were hot mineral springs whose water could be drunk only if very hot. When lukewarm, it became nauseating, as this church had become.
2. Spiritual poverty and self-deception (v. 17). The phrase "I am rich, and have become wealthy" implies that the church was boasting of getting her wealth by her own effort. In reality she was poor, blind, and naked, though she did not recognize her true state.

Exhortation, 3:18–19

The exhortation is for the church to find in Christ true riches ("gold refined by fire"), unfeigned purity ("white garments"), and spiritual sight to see her true condition. The reference to eye salve alludes to the medicine made in Laodicea, which was to be smeared on the eyes.

Promise, 3:20–22

It seems unbelievable that Christ should be outside the door of His own church, but this is exactly what verse 20 pictures. Yet He still extends His offer of grace to any individual who will invite Him into his or her heart. When the Savior comes in, He will take whatever the individual offers ("dine with him") and give to the individual all the riches that He has to offer ("and he with Me"). Then to that believer is promised true exaltation in association with Christ in His millennial rule (v. 21).

47

Summary

What are some of the universal lessons we can learn from these seven letters? (1) Times and churches have not changed much. Coolness and compromise are there on the part of some, as well as good works and faithfulness on the part of others. (2) The culture in which we live often rubs off on our church life—usually not for good. (3) The Lord is more interested in developing our character than in the routine continuing of our performance. (4) Christ is not only the head of the universal church, which is His body, but He is also the head of local churches, walking in their midst and concerned about their direction and conduct. Regrettably, however, local churches can ignore or push aside their Lord and go their own ways—but, of course, not without His knowing what is going on.

THE THRONE
IN HEAVEN

4:1–11

....

SECTION 3:
"THE THINGS WHICH SHALL TAKE PLACE,"
4:1–22:21

Chapter 4 begins the third main section of the book, being introduced with the same words as were used in the outline in 1:19 ("after these things," *meta tauta*). This entire portion is divided into three principal sections: the Tribulation period (4:1–19:21); the Millennium (20:1–15); and the eternal state (21:1–22:21). Chapters 4 and 5 form a prologue to the entire section. It was necessary that John be given a glimpse of the throne in heaven before witnessing the terrible judgments to be poured out on the earth. In other words, he was given a heavenly perspective on the coming earthly events as he walked through the door that was opened to him in 4:1.

The word "door" is used only four times in the entire book. In 3:8 there is a door of opportunity for service for the church in Philadelphia. In 3:20 (where the word is used twice) the opening of the door of the heart brings salvation and fellowship. Here the door opened to John brought heavenly insights on this earthly scene, a necessary and helpful prerequisite to understanding the purposes of God. The words "come up here" indicate John's personal transferral from earth to heaven. They do not specifically teach the Rapture of the church, although in the pretribulational understanding of prophecy the Rapture would occur at this point in the book. In support of this is the absence from this point on of any mention of churches, suggesting that believers of this church age are absent from the earth because of a pretribulational Rapture. In a postribulational view, of course, believers remain on the earth during the entire tribulation period and are not raptured until immediately before the Second Coming in chapter 19.

The Person on the Throne, 4:2–3

When John arrived in heaven he was immediately in the spirit (1:10), a state of spiritual sensitivity to receive the visions. The first thing he saw was the throne. Revelation can well be called the throne book, the word "throne" being used forty-five times, compared to only fifteen other occurrences of the word in the rest of the New Testament. The "One sitting [the present participle in both verses 2 and 3 indicates continuous occupancy] on the throne" is identified as God in verse 8. His appearance is compared to two precious stones. Revelation 21:11 explains that "jasper" is a crystal, that is, the color of light. The "sardius" stone, named for the city of Sardis where it was found, is blood red.

The Picture Connected with the Throne, 4:3, 5–6

Around The Throne, 4:3

Around the throne was a rainbow the light green color of an emerald. The color may suggest a mediating between the brilliant colors of jasper and sardius stones, but the rainbow itself was a vivid reminder of the faithfulness of God (Gen. 9:11–17). In this instance the rainbow is a sign not of His faithfulness never to flood the earth again but of His promise to give our Lord His rightful inheritance of ruling over this earth (Pss. 2:8–9; 110). Unlike the natural phenomenon of rainbows, of which we usually see only a part, this heavenly rainbow completely encircles the throne of God, thus emphasizing the completeness of His faithfulness.

Out of the Throne, 4:5

From the throne came lightnings, thunderings, and voices. These seem to be portents of judgments and are found again in 8:5; 11:19; and 16:18.

Before the Throne, 4:5–6

Before the throne were seven lamps of fire. They are interpreted as the "seven Spirits of God" or the fullness of the Holy Spirit (as in 1:4; 3:1; 5:6). Also before the throne (the same preposition is used) was a sea of glasslike crystal. What John saw is comprehensible; its significance, though, may not be so clear. Swete thinks that it "suggests the vast distance which, even in the case of one who stood at the door of heaven, intervened between himself and the Throne of God."[1] Strauss contrasts it with the laver in the tabernacle, which was for cleansing. He notes that in heaven the sea is solidified, indicating that the saints have attained a fixed state of holiness without further need of cleansing (cf. 15:2).[2]

The Elders around the Throne, 4:4

Their Identification

The persons around the throne are described as "twenty-four elders." Some, such as W. R. Newell[3] are convinced that these are twenty-four heavenly beings of an angelic order that is associated with God's government in some special way. Most other pre-millennial writers understand them to be twenty-four redeemed human beings around the throne who, though individuals, represent all the redeemed. In the New Testament, elders, as the highest officials in the church, do represent the whole church (cf. Acts 15:6; 20:28), and in the Old Testament, twenty-four elders were appointed by King David to represent the entire Levitical priesthood (1 Chron. 24). When those twenty-four elders met together in the temple precincts in Jerusalem, the entire priestly house was represented. Thus it seems more likely that the elders represent redeemed human beings, not angels.

Some understand the twenty-four to be divided into two groups of twelve each, one group representing the redeemed of the Old Testament and the other the redeemed of the New Testament church. Others do not include the Old Testament saints at all, but see the twenty-four elders as representing the church only.[4] This appears to be more probable, since it is likely that redeemed Israelites will not be resurrected until the second coming of Christ, at the conclusion of the Tribulation (Dan. 12:2). By either understanding, the church is in heaven before the Tribulation begins.

Their Coronation

The elders are seated "on thrones" (not "seats," as in the KJV) and are crowned with gold crowns. The word for "crown" *(stephanos)* is used of the believers' rewards in 1 Corinthians 9:25; 1 Thessalonians 2:19; 2 Timothy 4:8; James 1:12; 1 Peter 5:4 and seems to be another indication that the twenty-four elders are human, not angelic, beings. Furthermore, crowns are never promised to angels.

Their Clothing

These saints are clothed in white raiment. This type of dress is attributed to saints, not angels, elsewhere in Revelation (3:5, 18).

Praise to God on the Throne, 4:6–11

By the Living Ones, 4:6–9

In verse 6 we are introduced to another group in connection with the throne: the "four living creatures." The word means "living ones" and does not of itself indicate whether they were animal, human, angelic, or divine. Many believe that they are cherubim, since Ezekiel writes of "living ones" and identifies them as cherubim (Ezek. 10:15, 20). Others think these living ones are manifestations or attributes of God Himself, who is on the throne. They are said to be "in the center" of the throne—something not said about anyone or anything else in this chapter. But they are also said to be "around the throne" (as are the rainbow and the elders). Their identification may not be able to be determined with certainty, but what they do is quite clear.

Each one is different in appearance. It would be difficult to ignore the similarity between the four living ones and the four-fold manner in which Christ is represented in the gospels. "Like a lion" pictures His kingship as particularly emphasized by Matthew. "Like a calf," that is, the sacrificial animal (Heb. 9:12, 19), reminds one of Mark's emphasis. "A face like that of a man" is obviously akin to Luke's emphasis on the humanity of Christ, and a "flying eagle" links Him with heaven, as John does.

The living ones' praise of God is ceaseless ("day and night"). They ascribe to God holiness (cf. Isa. 6:3), total authority ("Almighty" literally means "all-ruler"), eternality, glory, and honor (v. 9). They also offer thanks to God. Glory and honor have to do with the perfections of God, while thanks refers to His gifts in creation and redemption.

By the Twenty-Four Elders, 4:10–11

The elders who have been seated on their thrones (cf. v. 4) rise and prostrate themselves before God. The word "worship" means "to prostrate oneself before one whose worth is acknowledged" (the English word was originally "worthship"). As a further act of homage, they cast their crowns before God and praise Him in the words of verse 11. They address the One on the throne as the Lord and "our God" (in some texts, though omitted in the KJV). They ascribe to Him glory, honor, and power. They attribute to Him not only the creation of all things but the motivation for creating all things ("because of [Your] will"). His will is the cause of Creation, and He Himself is the Agent of it.

If the living ones are cherubim, then the scene is one of the redeemed (as represented by the twenty-four elders) joining with the cherubim (representing all the elect angels) in magnifying the worth of the Creator-God. If the living ones represent the attributes of God, then the elders are seen responding with worship to this revelation of His attributes. In either case, the glory of the elders falls before the glory of God. Casting our crowns before Him demonstrates that everything that we have and have accomplished as redeemed people is a gift of His grace, according to the pleasure of His own will. In heaven we will acknowledge this. It is tragic that we do not do it sooner.

THE SEVEN-SEALED
BOOK

5:1–14

....

Chapters 4 and 5 are a unit since they describe the scene in heaven, which gave John the proper perspective on the judgments to follow. In chapter 4 the focus of attention is on the throne and its occupant; in chapter 5 it is on the book (scroll) and its recipient.

Description of the Book, 5:1

Its Placement

The book (scroll) was in the right hand of God on the throne when John first saw it (though it was later removed from that place, v. 7).

Its Description

The book was most likely a scroll rather than a codex like our modern books (cf. *biblion* in v. 1 with Luke 4:17, 20; 2 Tim. 4:13). It was sealed securely with seven seals along one edge of the scroll. Although the contents of the scroll were not then known, it was so full that the writing overflowed to the back side as well.

Its Contents

Actually, we are not told in this chapter what the scroll contained, but when the seals are broken in chapter 6 the judgments of God are poured out on the earth. When the seventh seal is opened (8:1), the trumpets sound, and when the seventh trumpet blows, Christ is said to receive the kingdoms of this world (11:15).

Thus the scroll seems to contain the story of humanity's losing its lordship over creation and the regaining of that authority by the man Christ Jesus. The scroll might be titled the "Book of Redemption" since it contains the story of redemption to its final consummation, not only in relation to humanity but also in relation to the world. Satan had usurped what God originally gave to humanity in Adam, and Christ the Redeemer reclaimed cursed humanity and the cursed earth (cf. Heb. 2:5–9).

The Problem Related to the Book, 5:2–5

The Problem, 5:2

The problem was to find someone who was worthy to open the scroll.

The Reactions, 5:3–4

First, there was a search, which yielded no one able to break the seals and open the scroll. The threefold characterization of the universe in verse 3 is the same as in Philippians 2:10. This failure to find any qualified person shows the complete helplessness of humankind. Second, there was sorrow and sobbing on the part of John, because it appeared as if there were no one who could redeem the inheritance. The weeping continued (imperfect tense in v. 4) until one of the elders stopped John and announced that Christ would open the scroll. He is the Lion of the tribe of Judah (cf. Gen. 49:8–10), the Root of David, and the heir to the throne and promises made to David (2 Sam. 7; Matt. 22:42–43; Luke 1:31–33). Both descriptions emphasize Christ's kingship as the noblest Son (Lion) of the kingly tribe (Judah) and as the One greater than King David who will ultimately fulfill the promises of the Davidic covenant by ruling on the throne of David in the millennial kingdom.

The Recipient of the Book, 5:6–14

Revealed, 5:6–7

The Lion is now revealed as a Lamb, but the fourfold description scarcely fits the usual image of a lamb!

The Lamb. He is standing in the midst of the throne. A standing lamb is a contradiction of ideas, but well represents the majesty and meekness of the Lamb of God. In heaven the Lord is seen both as seated (in relation to the finished aspect of His work of redemption) and as standing (in relation to the unfinished aspects of completing this redemption). Here He is standing ready to complete His work and assume the reins of power and government that are rightfully His.

The Lamb is slain. The emphasis is not on the Crucifixion, but on the Resurrection, since the slain Lamb is standing, not lying dead. This description also seems to indicate that the marks of His death remain unaltered throughout eternity to remind His people of the cost of their redemption.

The Lamb is strong. Horns are found everywhere in the Bible as a symbol of strength (1 Kings 22:11; Zech. 1:18). Death has not weakened Him.

The Lamb is scrutinizing. His seven eyes represent the fullness of the Spirit of God scrutinizing all the earth. It is this One who, not as an interloper but as the legitimate heir, takes the scroll out of the hand of God on the throne. This is one of the most climactic acts in all history, for it assures the regaining of all that was lost.

Revered, 5:8–14

At this point all creation bursts into praise for the Lamb who can open the scroll.

By the twenty-four elders, vv. 8–10, 14.

1. Their actions. The elders fall before the throne and worship (same word as in 4:10) the Lamb.
2. Their instruments. They have harps or lyres, the traditional instruments for praise (Pss. 33:2; 98:5). Along with these the prayers of the saints were offered as incense in bowls (an open vessel more like a saucer). The gender of the participle "holding" shows that the harps and bowls are used only by the elders and not by the living ones.
3. Their song. Their song magnifies the worth of the Lamb for four reasons:
   a. He was slain.
   b. That death ("with Your blood") brought redemption to people from every kindred, tongue, people, and nation.
   c. That redemption also resulted in a position before God as a kingdom of priests (cf. 1:5–6; 20:6).
   d. In the future (though some texts have a present tense of the verb here) the redeemed will reign on the earth—a reference to believers' participation in the millennial kingdom. In verses 9–10 there is also a textual problem as to whether the pronouns ought to be "us" or "them." If "us," then the elders are obviously singing of their own redemption and of those whom they represent; if "them," then they still could be singing of their own

redemption and those whom they represent in the third person instead of the first (as in Ex. 15:13, 15–17).

By angels, vv. 11–12. The angels (who are clearly distinguished here from the elders, indicating that the latter are not angels) join in praise to the Lamb. Nowhere in the Bible is it recorded specifically that angels sing. Here they cry with a loud voice. Their number is an innumerable multitude. They do not directly address the Lamb as did the elders, but they give to Him a sevenfold ascription of praise.

By every creature, v. 13. Every creature joins in the ascription of praise (Phil. 2:8–11).

By the living ones, v. 14. The four living ones respond to this hymn of adoration with an "Amen," closing this scene of universal homage to the One who is the focus of all God's purposes for time and eternity.

THREE SERIES OF JUDGMENTS

THE SEAL JUDGMENTS 6

1st – COLD WAR
2d – OPEN WAR
3d – FAMINE
4th – DEATH
5th – MARTYRDOM
6th – DISTURBANCES
7th – (8:1–6)

THE TRUMPET JUDGMENTS 8-9

1st – EARTH AFFECTED
2d – SEA AFFECTED
3d – WATERS AFFECTED
4th – HEAVENS AFFECTED
5th – MEN AFFECTED
6th – DEATH
7th – (11:15–19)

THE BOWL JUDGMENTS 16

1st – SORES
2d – SEA AFFECTED
3d – RIVERS AFFECTED
4th – SCORCHING
5th – DARKNESS
6th – EUPHRATES DRIED UP
7th – DESTRUCTION

THE SIX SEALS

6:1–17

....

Although the third and last principal section begins with 4:1, chapters 4 and 5 constitute a prologue to the judgments that begin to be poured out on the earth as described in chapter 6. Chapters 6–19 concern the events of the tribulation period, climaxing with the second coming of Christ in 19:11–16. There is no problem in outlining the events of these chapters; the difficulty comes in determining the sequential order of those events, particularly the relation of the three series of judgments to each other. Do the judgments of the seals (chap. 6) and the trumpets (chaps. 8–9) and the bowls (chap. 16) follow each other in succession, or do the trumpets and/or the bowls recapitulate with greater intensity the judgments of the seals? In other words, do the trumpet and bowl judgments follow the seals as different and distinct judgments, or do they picture the same judgments? In this writer's understanding they all follow in chronological sequence, and there is no recapitulation.[1] However, this does not mean that these judgments are equally spaced throughout the entire seven years of tribulation. The bowl judgments, for example, appear to occur rapidly one after the other. In this book the chronological sequence is based on the premise that the judgments are sequential and that chapters

6, 8–9, and 16 form the chronological framework of this section.

The other chapters in this section (besides 6, 8–9, and 16) relate events most important to our understanding of the Tribulation, but not necessarily in chronological order. Some commentators call them parentheses, which is a perfectly proper word and does not connote unrelatedness or unimportance. These chapters contain fill-in materials that are vital to the complete picture, but they are not necessarily arranged chronologically.

To summarize: chapters 6–19, which picture the tribulation period, contain three series of judgments: the seals (6), the trumpets (8–9), and the bowls (16). These follow one another in order. The other chapters reveal vital information about the period but are not arranged in chronological order. They sometimes cover the entire period (chap. 7) or spotlight an event within the period (chap. 18) or survey the first or last half of the period (chap. 11). The chapters in this section are not unlike a conversation on the telephone between two persons. They start telling the story in order (chap. 6), but soon there is an interruption to fill in some information (chap. 7). Then the order of events is resumed (chaps. 8–9) only to return to some more fill-in (chaps. 10–15). There is a return to the progressive order of events (chap. 16) and finally more detail (chaps. 17-19). Sometimes the "fill-in" material runs ahead of the story; at other times it backs up to add or emphasize pertinent information. It may be helpful at this point to recapitulate the outline of Revelation used in this book.

   I. "The things which you have seen"(1:1–20)
  II. "The things which are"(2:1–3:22)
 III. "The things which shall take place after these things" (4:1–22:21)

Prologue (4:1–5:14)

A. The Tribulation (6:1–19:21)

    1. Seal Judgments (6:1–17) (Nonchronological information, 7:1–17)

    2. Trumpet Judgments (8:1–9:21) (Nonchronological information, 10:1–15:8)

    3. Bowl Judgments (16:1–21) (Nonchronological information, 17:1–19:21)

B. The Millennium (20:1–15)

C. The Eternal State (21:1–22:5)

Epilogue (22:6–21)

First Seal, 6:1–2

The first seal is opened by the Lamb, and the wrath of what one normally considers a docile being begins to be revealed. The opening of the first seal reveals to John a white horse and rider. Some interpret the rider of the white horse to be Christ because of 19:11, but the only similarity between the two passages is the white horse. Other judgments do not follow in chapter 19 as they do in chapter 6; the crown the rider wears in 6:2 *(stephanos)* is different from that in 19:12 *(diadēma),* and the appearance of Christ on earth at this point in the book is incongruous. The rider is Antichrist who goes forth conquering at the very beginning of the tribulation period. The method of conquest at this time, however, does not seem to be by open hostilities, for peace is not removed from the earth until the second seal is opened. One might label this judgment, then, "cold war," and this corresponds perfectly with the delusion of peace and safety at the beginning of the Tribulation, as stated in 1 Thessalonians 5:3.

Second Seal, 6:3–4

In interpreting this book it is always a wise procedure to move from the clearer statements to the less clear. It is perfectly clear that, in the judgment of the second seal, peace is removed from the earth and people begin open war with each other. Phrases in verse 4 explicitly state this, and the statement "a great sword was given to him" confirms it. That also shows that all is within God's control. The red color of the horse also suggests bloodshed.

Third Seal, 6:5–6

The third judgment brings famine to the world. The black horse forebodes death, and the parity of balances bespeaks a careful rationing of food. Normally a denarius, which was a day's wages for a rural worker in Palestine in Jesus' day (Matt. 20:2), would buy ten quarts of wheat or thirty of barley. Under these famine conditions, the same wage will buy only one quart of wheat or three of barley. In other words, there will be one-tenth the normal supply of food. One quart of wheat was the daily ration for a soldier. At this point in the Tribulation, a daily wage will buy food for only one person. How will families survive? The phrase "do not damage the oil and the wine" is an ironic twist in this terrible situation. Apparently, luxury food items will not be in short supply, but of course most people will not be able to afford them. This situation will only serve to taunt the populace in their impoverished state.

Fourth Seal, 6:7–8

The color of the fourth horse is "ashen" or, better, "yellowish-green." The same word is used in 9:4 of green vegetation. This rider only among the four horsemen is named, and he is called Death. Death claims the physical part of a person (the immaterial never dies) and is accompanied by Hades, which claims the immaterial part. Here is evidence that death does not end all, for the soul goes to Hades at death, and eventually the unsaved person will be cast into the Lake of Fire (20:14). The effect of this judgment is that one-fourth of the population of the earth is killed (cf. 9:18, where an additional one-third are killed). The means of extermination are four: sword (war), hunger (famine that often follows war), death (perhaps by plagues of disease that often accompany war), and wild beasts of the earth (which apparently will be unrestrained and will roam the earth to kill people). Suddenly all human programs for bringing in peace, plenty, and longevity through medicine will be overturned in the short time that it will take to accomplish this judgment (cf. Matt. 24:4–7).

Fifth Seal, 6:9–11

The fifth seal depicts actions in heaven that result from certain happenings on earth. Attention has previously been focused on events that will occur on the earth. Now it shifts to a group of martyrs in heaven, and, of course, they are in heaven because of having been martyred on the earth. Who are these people? They are not the martyrs of the Church Age, for church saints are raptured before the holocaust of the Tribulation begins. They must be those who were saved after the Rapture and then martyred during these first months of the Tribulation, when the judgments of the first four seals were being poured out. The reason for their being slain is plain: because of the Word of God and their testimony (v. 9b). Literally, the text says "for the witness which they were having" (imperfect tense). In other words, they are faithful witnesses during the early days of the Tribulation when people, though experiencing these awful judgments, will still not turn to God. In their wrath these vile people will kill God's witnesses.

As soon as they die they are received into heaven, and they are pictured here to John as under the altar (i.e., they had already been offered as a sacrifice). They wear white robes (cf. 7:9; 19:8), signifying their fully redeemed state, and they cry for vengeance on those who killed them. They address God as "Lord" (Despot, v. 10), a word which shows recognition of His absolute control over all the affairs of the world.

The Lord's answer to them (v. 11) is that they should wait a little while for vengeance, until certain others should be martyred also. God's reply provides a glimpse into the complicated problems of why evil is allowed to reign. God simply allows it for His own purposes, which are best from the viewpoint of His total plan, though difficult to understand from our limited viewpoint. It was difficult for these martyrs to understand why God would allow these evil murderers to live, but He asks them to trust Him to work out all things in the best way.

Sixth Seal, 6:12–17

Apparently following immediately, the judgment of the sixth seal unleashes universal havoc on the earth. Six catastrophic events will be involved: (1) A great earthquake will occur. Three other earthquakes are mentioned later (8:5; 11:13; 16:18–19). (2) The sun will be darkened so that it becomes black as sackcloth. Remember, it is very important to notice the words "as" and "like" in interpreting the book. The sun will not be turned into sackcloth, but will be blackened *as* sackcloth. (3) The moon will become red *as* blood. (4) There will be a meteor shower on the earth with great devastation. (5) Apparently heaven will be opened for a moment so that people on earth can have a glimpse of that awesome scene with God on His throne. (6) Every mountain and island will be moved to some extent. There is no "as" in this sentence.

The result of these judgments will be to strike terror into the hearts of people living on the earth. It is most interesting to note that what strikes fear in them will not be so much the physical disturbances in heaven and earth as the sight of God on the throne. People will plead to be hidden "from the presence of Him who sits on the throne, and from the wrath of the Lamb" (v. 16). They will go to any lengths to avoid God, even to seeking death from the rocks and mountains where they hide. This judgment has effects in all the world and among all classes of people (v. 15).

At this point humanity will know assuredly that this tribulation is uniquely different from all other periods of trouble and persecution that have come or will come upon the earth. Two characteristics show its difference. The first is that the judgments of the Tribulation are to be worldwide. All kinds of people throughout the earth (righteous remnant, sinners, and all social classes) will feel the judgments of that period. Also, when the Tribulation comes, people will not only know that the end of the world is near, but they will act like it. In every age there are those who predict the end of the world, but in no age have people acted as if they believed it would happen imminently. When the Tribulation comes, people will not be concerned with buying and selling real estate or saving and planning for the future; according to these verses they will dig out caves in the mountains and rocks and seek death, not the prolonging of life. This is an awesome scene, but if language means anything, the picture is plain.

THE REDEEMED
OF THE TRIBULATION

7:1–17

....

The narrative sequence is interrupted at this point in Revelation, for chapter 6 closed with a description of the sixth seal, and the seventh seal is not opened until the beginning of chapter 8. Although in a sense chapter 7 is a parenthesis, it is also a very logical interlude in the account. From the severity of the judgments under the sixth seal, it would appear that not a single person could or would be saved. "For the great day of their wrath has come; and who is able to stand?" (6:17). But even in the wrath of the Tribulation, God remembers mercy. So the scene of judgment is interrupted by the scene of mercy in this chapter.

Sealing of 144,000 Jews, 7:1–8

Suspension of Judgment 7:1–3

Instruments of the suspension, vv. 1–2. In suspending judgment for a time God will use angels. Scarcely any person appreciates the extent of the ministry of angels. It is not that God requires their service, but He chooses to use them in the execution of His plans. In Revelation, angels are used both in executing judgments (as in 8:2) and in halting judgment (as here in 7:1–3). In addition to the reference to the angels of the churches in Revelation 2–3 (which may be angels or human messengers), there are sixty-seven other occurrences of the word in this book. John first saw four angels standing at the four "corners" of the earth (i.e., at the four quadrants or directions of the compass). They apparently control the winds (cf. the angel of fire, 14:18; and the angel of the waters, 16:5), preventing them from blowing on the earth, which would result in a lack of rain on the earth. Then John saw a fifth angel, who came from the East (literally, "the rising of the sun"). He was also given a special mission in relation to the 144,000.

Instruction concerning suspension, vv. 2–3. This fifth angel appears to be superior to the other four. This is not strange, for other Scriptures demonstrate that there are ranks among both the good and evil angels (Eph. 3:10; 6:12). He instructs the four to suspend judgment, but he also associates them with him in the sealing ("until *we* have sealed," v. 3b). His crying with a loud voice may emphasize the urgency of this project. The instructions are clear: suspend judgment temporarily.

Intent of the suspension, v. 3. The purpose of the suspension is that a certain group may be sealed. These "bond-servants of our God" are described in detail in verses 4–8. They are Jews from each of the twelve tribes, and they do a particular service for God. In some way they are sealed on their foreheads. Whether a visible mark or characteristic of some kind is involved is not stated or implied in the text. Some suggest something visible after the manner of Ezekiel 9:4, or like the glory with which Moses's face shone, or like the mark Antichrist will place on unbelievers (13:16). But a seal does not have to be visible to be real (Eph. 4:30). It is principally a guarantee of ownership and security, and both these ideas are evident in the sealing of these 144,000. They are owned by God, which must indicate that they are redeemed people. And they are kept secure by God, which means that they have physical safety from their enemies on the earth while they are accomplishing their service for the Lord. It is commonly assumed that their service includes evangelism, though this is not specifically stated.

Sum of the Jews, 7:4–8

Although some interpret this list as indicating only in a very general sense the preservation of believers during trials at any time, and others as the sealing of the church, if language is to be understood normally, the list is of 144,000 Jews. The repetitious "from the tribe of . . . were sealed" is too ringing to allow any other conclusion. Anyone today who claims to be among this group would have to know to what tribe he or she belonged. A. J. Seiss wrote,

> Nor is there a vice or device of sacred hermeneutics, which so beclouds the Scriptures, and so unsettles the faith of men, as this constant attempt to read Church for Israel, and Christian peoples for Jewish tribes. As I read the Bible, when God says "children of Israel," I do not understand Him to mean any but people of Jewish blood, be they Christians or not; and when He speaks of the twelve tribes of the sons of Jacob and gives the names of the tribes, it is impossible for me to believe that He means the Gentiles, in any sense or degree, whether they be believers or not.[1]

The identification of these people imposes no obstacle if the language is understood plainly. But there are three problems in this list.

The first is the inclusion of Levi among the twelve tribes. Normally Levi, being the priestly tribe, was considered to have no separate inheritance among the twelve tribes, though they were given cities among all of the other tribal areas. Perhaps Levi is included here because the priests were the spiritual leaders of the nations.

The second is the mention of Joseph instead of Ephraim. Normally Manasseh and Ephraim are both mentioned since they both received an equal portion of territory along with the rest of the tribes. Of course, a double number is counted in this list, but under the names of Joseph and Manasseh rather than Ephraim and Manasseh.

The third problem concerns the omission of Dan from this list, something that was necessary if Levi were to be included. The usual reason given for this omission is that Dan was guilty of idolatry on many occasions (Lev. 24:11; Judg. 18:1–2, 30–31; 1 Kings 12:28–29). The same reason is often given for the omission of Ephraim. Some have suggested further that the Antichrist may come from this tribe and that that accounts for its omission from the list (cf. Gen. 49:17; Jer. 8:16). Whatever the reason for Dan's omission from the list of tribes from which the 144,000 elect will come, this is not the end of God's dealings with that tribe. The Danites will receive a portion of the land during the millennial kingdom. Indeed, in Ezekiel 48:1 Dan heads the list of the tribes as the inheritance is divided to them (cf. also 48:32). So the exclusion here is not permanent, for the gifts and calling of God with regard to His people, including Dan, are without repentance.

Saving of Many Gentiles, 7:9–17

The Persons Saved, 7:9

Their number. Verse 9 introduces a new vision with the words "after these things." John saw a group different in several ways from the 144,000. He described this group literally as "a great multitude." This is an innumerable group, not a definite number like the 144,000.

Their nationalities. The 144,000 are all Israelites. This group is composed of many nationalities.

Their nature. They are described as wearing white robes and holding palms in their hands. In other words, they are redeemed and rejoicing. The word for "robes" is "stoles"—white stoles finer than the finest white ermine or mink and indicative of a far more important possession, salvation. The palms apparently denote rejoicing and victory (cf. John 12:13 for the only other occurrence in the New Testament, and Neh. 8:15).

Praise for Their Salvation, 7:10–12

The redeemed multitude cry an ascription of praise to God and to the Lamb for their salvation (v. 10). The angels, the four living ones, and the elders respond by worshiping God. The angels, of course, do not personally experience salvation, but they rejoice in the salvation of sinners (cf. Luke 15:8–10).

Period Of Their Salvation, 7:13–14

John was evidently puzzling over the identity of this group (scarcely imaginable if the group were the church saints), and God, who knows our thoughts, answered his perplexity through one of the elders. They are explicitly identified as "the ones who come out of the great tribulation."

> That they are distinct from the church appears from the following considerations: Believers living at the time of the rapture of the church will have no place or part in the tribulation; these people will live during some of the tribulation days,

be killed, and received into heaven. Those wear white garments
(4:4); these white robes. Those sit on thrones round about
the throne; these stand before the throne. Those wear crowns;
these are uncrowned. Those have harps and vials; these have
palms in their hands. Those sing a new song; these cry with a
loud voice. Those are kings and priests and reign with Him;
these serve Him day and night.[2]

Many of these will doubtless be saved through believing the
message by means of media and literature that are left after the
Rapture and/or through the service (evangelism) of the 144,000.

The Provisions of Salvation, 7:15–17

Their service, v. 15. This group (along with others) will serve
God. "In His temple" likely indicates some special service for
them in the yet future millennial temple.

Their satisfaction, vv. 15–16. They are satisfied because of the
presence of God. God's sheltering, shepherding, protecting care is
their portion. They are satisfied because of the provisions of God
(v. 16), which include no hunger, no thirst, no exposure.

Their sufficiency, v. 17. Sufficiency from the shepherding ministry of the Lamb is the final provision. The mention of eternal life
brings the additional assurance of no tears. The Lamb in this scene
is not only the satisfaction and sufficiency of these redeemed, but
also His presence is security. In turn, the redeemed serve Him
without interruption.

Both these groups in Revelation 7—the 144,000 and the saved
multitude who are largely Gentiles—demonstrate clearly that the
Tribulation will be a period of salvation for many people. Even
though the body of saints known as the church will be completed
and raptured (and thus the Holy Spirit's residence in the world

will in a special sense be withdrawn), God will not cease to save those who believe in His Son. The activity of the grace of God will not cease as long as time continues.

THE SEVENTH SEAL AND THE FIRST FOUR TRUMPETS

8:1–13

....

The interlude recorded in chapter 7 has concluded and the pouring out of judgments on the earth resumes.

OPENING OF THE SEVENTH SEAL, 8:1

With the opening of this last seal the book is now fully opened, and one would expect a holocaust to let loose. Instead, there is silence. All of the choruses of the elders and the cries of the angels cease. The stillness is so intense that it can be felt. This is a silence of expectancy, for this is the last seal. It is also a silence of foreboding that precedes the onslaught of judgments. It lasts for half an hour (which may be understood just as literally as the other time designations in the book). Silence at this point, after all the vocal expressions of worship previously noted, would be an awesome thing.

With the opening of this seal comes the series of trumpet judgments. It has already been stated that I view these series of judgments as successive, in which case the trumpets come out of and follow the seals. This seems to be the simplest way to understand these judgments, although others feel that there is overlapping and recapitulation.[1]

EIGHT ANGELS, 8:2–6

The Presence Angels, 8:2, 6

Their relationship. John first saw seven angels. They are a distinct group (the definite article is used) and they are before, or in the presence of, God. With the introduction of these angels, no further mention is made of the seven Spirits of God, which further indicates their special relationship to God and His purposes. (Could one of them be Gabriel, cf. Luke 1:26?)

Their responsibility. They are responsible for announcing the trumpet judgments, for the trumpets are given to them (v. 2). The sounding of trumpets is always followed by something of outstanding importance. The first occurrence was at the giving of the law (Ex. 19:16; 20:18; cf. Jer. 4:5; 1 Cor. 15:51–52; 1 Thess. 4:16).

The Priest Angel, 8:3–5

Before the sounding of the trumpets, an interlude occurs with the appearance of another angel. His function as a priest is clear; his identification is less certain. Some understand this to be Christ, our High Priest (cf. 1 Tim. 2:5).[2] Others regard him as an angel,[3] and there seems to be no reason why an angel could not perform the functions described here. He adds incense to the prayers of the saints that ascend before God. Though the imagery is of the tabernacle worship, the meaning is now clearer in light of the finished work of Christ. The incense is the sweet savor of His life and work, which gives efficacy to the prayers of the saints.

Who are the saints whose prayers are being heard here? At the very least they are saints of the Tribulation who are living on the earth and who pray to God for an outpouring of His wrath on the godless rebels on the earth. But they may include the saints of all time whose longing petitions for the coming of the Lord's kingdom are now about to be answered. In any case, their prayers are heard, angels being involved in the hearing and answering but always on the basis of the merit of the Savior.

After prayer ascends, judgment descends (v. 5). The angel fills his censer with fire from the altar (not the golden altar before the throne but the bronze altar of judgment), and he casts it onto the earth. There follows a token or preview judgment: voices, thunderings, lightnings, and an earthquake—a foretaste of the trumpet judgments to follow. The action of the priest angel gives the signal to the presence angels to sound the trumpets.

First Four Trumpets, 8:7–13

First Trumpet, 8:7

The first trumpet will bring hail and fire mingled with blood on the earth. The result will be the burning up of a third part of the earth (reliable texts include this phrase in v. 7), a third part of the trees and all the grass. This shows clearly that God is in complete control, allowing the judgment to affect only one-third of the earth and trees but all of the grass.

Commentators who hold to the futuristic interpretation of this book are divided over the extent to which these judgments should be understood plainly. Some see the words "trees," "grass," "sea," and "ships" as symbols. For instance, Walter Scott understands the third part of the earth to mean the devastation of the Western confederation of nations, the third part of the trees to be the leaders and great men of the world, and the grass to represent people in general.[4] Of course, symbols are often used in this book, but they are so stated. Here there is no indication that these are symbols, so it seems better to understand them plainly.

This is not a question of literal versus figurative interpretation. It is a question of the extent to which symbols are being used within the framework of literal or plain interpretation of the book. Consistent interpretation in relation to the language of these verses would seem to rule out any symbols here. As has often been pointed out, it would be very inconsistent to understand these judgments symbolically and yet interpret, say, the plagues in Egypt plainly and actually. The judgment of the first trumpet presents a grim picture of devastation on the vegetation of the world.

Second Trumpet, 8:8–9

The instrument of the second judgment is described as "something like a great mountain burning with fire." It is not necessary to attempt to find something in the realm of experience that can match this description. John really does not say what the instrument of judgment will be, but he clearly reveals its effect. A third part of the sea will become blood, causing the death of a third part of the life in the sea and the destruction of a third part of the shipping of the world. The bloody waters could come either from God's supernaturally changing the water into blood or from the blood of the dead animals. The far-reaching implications of such judgments are staggering to the mind. Concerning the destruction of marine organisms, for instance, Henry Morris says, "These constitute the lowest and most basic components of many of the world's food chains, so their destruction must produce a domino effect on many higher forms of life."[5]

Third Trumpet, 8:10–11

The judgment of the third trumpet affects one-third of the fresh water supply of the world (again reminding us that God is in complete control). The waters will become bitter (apparently lethal), causing many to die. The instrument of judgment will be a great star that is labeled Wormwood. "Many species of wormwood grow in Palestine. . . . All species have a strong, bitter taste, leading to the use of the plant as a symbol of bitterness, sorrow, and calamity."[6] Compare Proverbs 5:4 and Lamentations 3:15.

Fourth Trumpet, 8:12–13

The fourth judgment will affect the sun, moon, stars, and the uniformity of the day-night cycle. The sun, moon, and stars will be affected by one-third. This might mean one of two things: the twenty-four-hour cycle is reduced to sixteen hours, or the output of the power of the sun, moon, and stars is reduced by one-third. In either case, it would seem that this would cause a drop in temperature (but notice that the opposite occurs in 16:8–9). The Lord Himself predicted in the Olivet Discourse these "signs in the sun, and in the moon, and in the stars" (Luke 21:25). Perhaps this shortening of the days and nights is what is referred to in Matthew 24:22 (though, of course, that verse may mean that the total number of days is shortened).

At this point John heard and saw "an eagle" (not "angel" as in KJV) announcing woes to come. These will be inflicted on "those who dwell on the earth" (v. 13). The means of punishment will be the last three trumpets of the angels that were yet to sound. Terrible as the first four trumpet judgments will be, the last three will be worse and are thus designated "woes."

The warning is that trumpets five, six, and seven will bring a heightened degree of divine displeasure and consequent disasters. We shall see the first woe in the locusts (9:1–11); the second, the Euphrates horsemen and hosts (9:13–21) and the plagues wherewith the two witnesses (11:5–6) smite the earth. The third we see in the handing over of the earth to the Beast-worship of chapter 13—worst, by far, of all![7]

THE TRIBULATION JUDGMENTS
(REVELATION 8–9, 16)

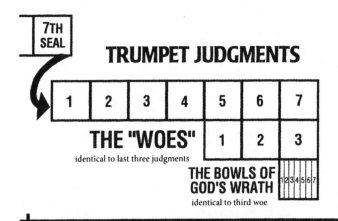

7TH
SEAL

TRUMPET JUDGMENTS

| 1 | 2 | 3 | 4 | 5 | 6 | 7 |

THE "WOES"
identical to last three judgments

| 1 | 2 | 3 |

THE BOWLS OF
GOD'S WRATH
identical to third woe

| 1 | 2 | 3 | 4 | 5 | 6 | 7 |

SECOND HALF OF THE TRIBULATION

WOES ON THE EARTH

9:1–21

....

First Woe—Fifth Trumpet, 9:1–12

Like arrows from a bow, the locusts of judgment of the first woe are discharged upon the earth.

Destruction by the Locusts, 9:1–6

The agent who discharged them, v. 1. When the fifth angel sounded his trumpet, John saw a star. He is described as having "fallen" (not "fall" as KJV) to the earth. In other words, John did not see the star actually fall; it had already fallen.

Who or what is this star? Sometimes the word "star" refers to a heavenly body (as in 8:12). But the word is often used to refer to some kind of intelligent creature, usually an angel (cf. 1:20; Job 38:7). Both meanings are perfectly consistent with plain, normal interpretation. For example, in English we use this word in the same two ways. Literally, a star means an astronomical entity; and as a figure of speech, we use the word to mean a person, like the star of a football game. In these verses the star is an intelligent creature who performs certain responsible actions.

Can the creature be identified further? He is obviously a creature with great authority to be able to hold captive and then unleash these locusts. He apparently is the same creature who in verse 11 is called the "angel of the abyss." Some identify this angel as Satan. Whether an angel or Satan, his great authority includes having a key to the bottomless pit; yet that authority is delegated to him by God and is restricted by the One who has "the keys of death and of Hades" (1:18) and who eventually will confine Satan to that same Abyss (20:3).

The area from which they are discharged, v. 2. They come from this Abyss. Literally, the phrase is "shaft of the abyss" in both verses 1 and 2. The word "abyss" occurs in Revelation seven times (9:1–2, 11; 11:7; 17:8; 20:1, 3) and elsewhere only twice (Luke 8:31; Rom. 10:7). The use of the word "shaft" gives the picture of a pit entered by a shaft or well that is guarded under lock and key. Luke 8:31 shows that the Abyss is the abode of demons. When the angel/star opens the pit, smoke ascends as from a great furnace. There are more occurrences of the words "as" and "like" here than in any other chapter in the Bible. This shows how difficult it was for John to describe the scene he saw in the vision. So dense was the smoke that the sun and air were darkened.

Their activity, vv. 3–6. Out of the smoke came locusts onto the earth. The description that follows in verses 6–11 shows that these will not be ordinary locusts, and their origin from the shaft of the Abyss substantiates that conclusion. These creatures are described as being very real, so we must not consider them as merely "symbolic representations of judgment." They are animal creatures, like locusts, though not ordinary locusts, for they are demonic in nature. Indeed, it would be better to describe them as demons who take the form of these unique locusts. Verse 11 makes clear that this is the case.

1. The description, v. 3. The destruction these demon-insects inflict is described to be like that of scorpions.

The pain from the sting of a scorpion, though not generally fatal, is perhaps, the [most intense] that any animal can inflict upon the human body. The insect itself is the most irascible and malignant that lives, and its poison is like itself. Of a boy stung in the foot by a scorpion [it was related that] . . . he rolled on the ground, grinding his teeth, and foaming at the mouth. It was a long time before his complaining moderated, and even then he could make no use of his foot, which was greatly inflamed. And such is the nature of the torment which these locusts from the pit inflict. They are also difficult to be guarded against, if they can be warded off at all, because they fly where they please, dart through the air, and dwell in darkness.[1]

In one locust plague it was estimated that 130 million locusts per square mile covered the ground! If there will be even one-hundreth as many in this judgment, with bites like scorpions, the intensity and pain of it is beyond imagination. (See also 1 Kings 12:14, where Rehoboam said he would discipline the people with the intensity of scorpions.)

2. The limitations, vv. 4–5. Horrible as the torment will be, God will place certain limitations on the activity of these demons. They will be limited as to *what* they may strike, *how far* they may go, and *how long* they may do what they do. They will not attack the vegetation of the earth (as common locusts do); they may attack only certain people, that is, those who do not have the seal of God on their foreheads (the 144,000; cf. 7:3–4). The wicked will persecute God's servants (the 144,000) but in turn they will be tormented by this plague that God allows. The demon-locusts will also be limited in that they may not kill people, just torment them. Further, the duration of this plague will be five months (cf. v. 10).

3. The effect, v. 6. The effect of this torment is to drive people to suicide, but they will not be able to die. Although they will prefer death to the agony of living, death will not be possible. Bodies will not sink and drown; poisons and pills will have no effect; and somehow even bullets and knives will not do their intended job.

Description of the Locusts, 9:7–11

As John now attempts to describe these uncommon locusts, these verses abound with the words of comparison—"as" and "like."

Their likeness, vv. 7–10. There are eight parts to the description, which begins with the head and progresses back to the tail of these creatures. Overall they are like horses prepared for battle (cf. Joel 2:4). On their heads were what appeared to be "crowns like gold." Their faces were "like the faces of men," their hair "like the hair of women," their teeth like those of lions. They had breastplates "like breastplates of iron," and the sound of their wings was like chariots or horses going to battle.

Finally, the scorpion-like sting of their tails is mentioned again, along with the fact that this will be permitted to last only five months. Though it may be difficult for anyone to imagine such creatures, that is no reason to understand them as merely symbols. The power of demons is very great, and these uncommon locusts are demonic. Whatever the size and appearance of these creatures, one thing stands out in this description: they are ferocious in looks and actions. Little wonder this is called the first woe.

Although this judgment is literally hell on earth, the overruling power of God is interwoven throughout this passage. He allows this judgment to occur; He sets the limits on the destructive power of these demon-locusts; He brings it to a conclusion when His purpose in it is finished. He is in complete control.

Their leader, v. 11. These creatures are led in their work by a king—"the angel of the abyss." His name is given in both Hebrew and Greek and means "destroyer" in both languages. In this judgment he, through demons, will attempt to destroy people's bodies; he also destroys the souls of those who refuse to receive the Savior.

Second Woe—Sixth Trumpet, 9:13–21

The Command, 9:13–15

When the sixth angel sounded, a voice from the golden altar gave the command to him concerning this second woe. The golden altar is mentioned only here and in 8:3, and presumably the voice here in verse 13 belonged to the same priest angel introduced in 8:3. He commands the trumpet angel to loose the four angels who were bound and continue so to be (the tense is perfect) in the river Euphrates. Here are four good angels under the command of the priest angel loosing four evil angels who, up to this time, had been bound in the Euphrates. These evil angels were "prepared for the hour" (the definite article is in the text in v. 15) and for the purpose (Greek, *hina)* of killing a third of the human race. Again, one sees the sovereign hand of God working all these events for His own glory and in His own time. These demons who had been kept for this hour could not have released themselves or been freed by Satan until God gave the command.

Under the fourth seal judgment (6:8), one-fourth of the earth had been slain; now one-third. This means that these two judgments alone (to say nothing of the death caused by other wars and calamities) have reduced the population of the earth by one-half.

The Count, 9:16

An immense army of horsemen appear at this point, and the total number of them is 200 million. This army might be composed of humans or demons, or demon-possessed human beings. There are other examples in Scripture of supernatural armies (2 Kings 2:11; 6:13–17; Rev. 19:14). The weapons of this army are fire, smoke, and brimstone—the weapons of destruction and of hell, which may indicate that this army is composed of demons or demon-possessed humans.

The Characteristics, 9:17

The horses had heads like lions and tails like serpents (v. 19). The riders had breastplates of fire, hyacinth (a blue stone), and brimstone. From the mouths of the horses came the fire, smoke, and brimstone.

The Consequences, 9:18–21

"By these three plagues" means the fire, smoke, and brimstone (sulphur). The first consequence of the activity of this army from hell is that one-third of the population is destroyed. The second consequence concerns those who were not killed. One would expect that in the midst of all this suffering, people would turn to God and cry out for mercy. Instead, we read that they did not repent. In verses 20 and 21 is a description of the religion and life of unredeemed people on the earth during these tribulation days. Their religion will be the worship of demons (cf. 1 Tim. 4:1) and idols. Their life will be filled with murder, sorcery, fornication, and stealing. From the word for sorcery we derive in English the word "pharmacy." Sorcery, then, must include the misuse of drugs. Notice that three of these four practices are direct violations of three of the Ten Commandments (murder, fornication, stealing). Vice will reign in the place of virtue, as is necessarily the case since one's religion determines one's ethics. People in these days will have religion with many of its visible representations, but it will do nothing to change their lives.

At least three realities stand out from this chapter: (1) the reality and power of the unseen world of demons and Satan; (2) the reality of a God who judges; and (3) the reality of the hardness of sinful human hearts.

THE ANGEL
AND THE LITTLE
OPENED BOOK

10:1–11

....

The Character of the Angel, 10:1–2

The vision John received at this point is the longest in the book. Notice that the words "I saw" do not appear again until 13:1. This section also forms the longest interlude between judgments. Between the sixth and seventh seals came the sealing of the 144,000 and the salvation of the great multitude. Here, between the sixth and seventh trumpets, come a number of revelations before the sounding of that last trumpet.

The appearance of this angel must have been spectacular to John, for the angel had a number of unusual characteristics: (1) His origin was heavenly (v. 1). (2) He was glorious in appearance (v. 1); he was clothed with a cloud (often connected with the appearance of someone from heaven (Dan. 7:13; 1 Thess. 4:17); he had a rainbow on his head (as a crown); his face was as the sun in its brilliance; and his feet were as pillars in their stance. (3) The angel held a little book opened in his hand (v. 2). The form of the word "open" in verse 2 is perfect passive, indicating that the book had been already opened before it was seen by John at this point. That would indicate that this is not the same book as was seen sealed in chapter 5. The contents are revealed later in this chapter. (4) The angel took a stand with one foot on the sea and the other on the land (v. 2). This seems to present an image of conquest and to relate the angel and his ministry to God's purpose of taking possession of the entire world (land and sea), which will be worked out in the tribulation period.

What do these characteristics tell us about the identity of this angel? Some identify him with the Lord Jesus. The descent in a cloud (cf. Ps. 104:3), the face as the sun (cf. 1:16), the feet as pillars of fire (cf. 1:15), and the planting of his feet in an act of taking possession (1 Cor. 10:26) all point to the angel being Christ. Others, however, point out that an angel might have these characteristics as well. He is called a "strong" angel (the same word as in 5:2). Similar characteristics are ascribed to a man (clearly an angelic being) in Daniel 10:5–6. Furthermore, the archangel Michael's name means "who is like God," which would make these characteristics not unexpected. Also, there would be a problem in a descent of Christ at this point in the book (v. 1). There would be no problem, however, if this were an angel. It is quite possible that this angel is the same one who appeared in 8:3, the word "another" in 10:1 merely distinguishing him from the seven trumpet angels as it does in 8:3. In either identification he is a mighty being with great power and authority, whether His own as Christ or delegated to him as a mighty angel for use in accomplishing God's program.

The Cry of the Angel, 10:3–4

Its Character

The cry was "with a loud voice," like the roaring of a lion. The metaphor emphasizes the strength of the angel's voice.

Its Consequences

Two things followed. First, seven thunders uttered their voices, and, second, John was restrained from revealing what the thunders said. Thunders are usually harbingers of coming storms (as in 8:5); these were apparently connected with some of the judgments involved in God's gaining possession of the earth. But the specific details are not revealed, a voice from heaven (either God's or Christ's) forbidding John to do so.

Confirmation of the Angel, 10:5–7

The angel now confirms with an oath the purpose of God to take His rightful inheritance. He first takes the position of oathtaking (v. 5), raising his hand to heaven. The basis of his oath is God, who is described here as the eternal One and as the all-powerful Creator (v. 6). The fact that the angel does not swear by himself may indicate that he is not Christ. The affirmation made in the oath is that the mystery of God will be finished soon: "There will be delay no longer." The word translated "delay" is the word for "time." This translation is allowable,[1] though this is an interpretative translation based on the content of verse 7. The idea is that there will no longer be an interval of time, that is, a delay, because (v. 7) the mystery of God will be finished when the seventh angel sounds. This will be welcome news to the martyrs of the Tribulation, who are already in heaven awaiting God's vindication (6:9–11).

This expression, "the mystery of God," in this connection seems to indicate all the plans and purposes of God made known by Him to and through the Scriptures concerning His governmental proceedings with people on earth, looking always toward the establishment of the millennial kingdom under the rule of Christ. When Christ comes to take that kingdom, there will be no mystery, but, on the contrary, manifestation.[2]

A Command Involving the Angel, 10:8–10

Its Source, 10:8

The voice spoke to John. This is the same voice that forbade him to write the content of the thunders in verse 4.

Its Substance, 10:8

The voice commanded John to take the opened book from the angel's hand.

John's Obedience, 10:9–10

When John asked the angel for the book, the angel told him to eat it and predicted that it would be bitter in his stomach, though sweet to his taste. John obeyed and found it so (v. 10).

The Object, 10:9–10

What was the point of this? The opened book apparently contained revelations from God. It included some of the things John was about to write so that they would be revealed to us. Whether or not it contained all the remainder of the book of Revelation is of little consequence; it contained some of it at least. The point of this interlude—during which John was commanded to assimilate these prophecies before he wrote them—is simply that it is necessary for the prophet of God to let the Word of God affect him first before he ministers it to others.

This action is also a vivid picture of the truth that, although the fact of revelation may be pleasant to the taste, the contemplation or digestion of the truth may bring heaviness. This principle ought especially to be operative in our study of prophecy. Too often when one enters into an understanding of things to come, he or she never gets beyond the tasting stage. But, when the child of God digests all of the truth of the judgments to come, it can only bring heaviness of heart. Although John

> was doubtless delighted with the fact of a new revelation from the Lord, he nevertheless was distressed with the content of that revelation. While he doubtless rejoiced in a measure at the revelation of the coming triumph and glory, yet he was saddened and grieved because preceding that glory were to occur the most terrible judgments and martyrdoms in all history.[3]

As it was with John, so may it be with us.

The Commissioning of John, 10:11

Finally, John is commissioned. Whether this commission came from the angel or the voice of some unnamed source is neither obvious nor important. The commission is that the prophet "must [*dei,* "it is necessary to"] prophesy again." Full of the sweet taste and bitterness of the little book, necessity was laid upon him to prophesy. He is to prophesy "concerning many." The word "concerning" is *epi,* and it has several meanings. As Swete has said,

> The Seer is not sent to prophesy in their presence (epi with gen., cf. [Mk.] xiii.9 . . .), nor against them (epi with acc. . . .), but simply with a view to their several cases. . . . It is no one

Empire or Emperor that is concerned in the prophecies of the second half of the Apocalypse; not merely Rome or Nero or Domitian, but a multitude of races, kingdoms, and crowned heads.[4]

In other words, these prophecies concern many peoples, and this is the content of the little book.

THE TEMPLE, THE TWO WITNESSES, AND THE SEVENTH TRUMPET

11:1–19

....

The Temple, 11:1–2

John is no longer merely a witness of the action of these verses; he is a participant. He is instructed to measure the temple of God, and in order to do this "a measuring rod" is put into his hands. This was apparently a reed, a species of cane that grew in the Jordan Valley to a height of fifteen to twenty feet. This one was straight like a rod, though its length is not stated (Ezekiel's was six cubits, or about nine feet, Ezek. 40:5).

John was told to measure "the temple" *(naos,* the inner temple, or the Holy Place and the Holy of Holies), "the altar" (probably the altar of incense, which was in the holy place), and the worshipers. These worshipers are the faithful, believing Jews of the tribulation days. The temple is the one that will be built in Jerusalem (cf. v. 8) during the Tribulation and in which ancient

Jewish rites will be reinstituted. It is apparently the same temple
in which, at the middle of the Tribulation, the man of sin will
seat himself, demanding to be worshiped and overthrowing Jewish
worship (2 Thess. 2:4). The measuring itself seems to be an act
of knowing, claiming, or staking out. In this act of John's, God
is giving assurance that He will take note of those who faithfully
worship Him in the first half of the Tribulation.

The outer court of the Gentiles is not measured. Instead, John
is told to leave it out. The language indicates utter rejection, and
the reason is given: the Gentiles will tread underfoot the city of
Jerusalem for forty-two months. This will occur during the last part
of the Tribulation, when the man of sin overthrows Jewish worship
and demands worship of himself (Luke 21:24). Thus the func-
tioning worship of the temple described in 11:1–2 occurs during
the first part of the Tribulation, whereas the treading down of the
city by Gentiles (11:2) follows during the last forty-two months.

Two important spiritual principles are exhibited in these
verses: first, God is cognizant of all that is going on; second, God
determines the limits of persecution.

The Two Witnesses, 11:3–14

The Time of Their Ministry, 11:3

The time limit of the ministry of the two witnesses is stated
explicitly as 1,260 days. There is some disagreement over whether
this refers to the first or the last half of the Tribulation. The text
does not specify. It seems to me that it refers to the first half,
since it is the coming of the Beast (the Antichrist) onto the scene
with great power that terminates their witness (v. 7). Although
present and active during the first part of the Tribulation, chiefly
as a political figure, he does not show himself in his true character
and demand to be worshiped until the middle of the Tribulation.

At the midpoint he will kill the two witnesses who have been ministering during the first part of the Tribulation. If this is so, then, of course they will be witnessing along with the 144,000 during this time.

There will be three obstacles to Antichrist's ascendancy to a position of extraordinary power at the middle of the Tribulation: (1) the temple with its worship; (2) the two witnesses; and (3) the ecumenical church (chap. 17). All of these will be destroyed at the middle of the Tribulation, clearing the way for Antichrist to extend his plan to be a worldwide ruler.

The Traits of Their Ministry, 11:4–6

Their character, v. 4. These men are described as "two olive trees" and "two lampstands." The figure of olive trees comes from Zechariah 4:3, 14 and means that the witnesses are anointed ones. The figure of the two lampstands may also be from the same passage (where there is one lampstand and two pipes into which oil is poured and channeled to the lamps), and it evidently refers to the witnesses' character as bearers of the light of God's truth.

Their conduct, vv. 5–6. The conduct of their ministry is spectacular, to say the least. They will have power (1) to kill their enemies with fire, (2) to keep it from raining, (3) to turn the waters to blood (cf. 8:7–9), and (4) to bring plagues upon the earth (cf. 9:20). The first two are reminiscent of Elijah and the last two of Moses.

The Termination of Their Ministry, 11:7–10

The time, v. 7. Their ministry will be terminated only when "they have finished their testimony." They will be invincible until their work is done; only then will God permit them to be killed by Antichrist.

The means, v. 7. The means of their death will be the rise of "the beast that comes up out of the abyss." This is the first of thirty-six references to the Beast in the book. Martyrdom of the witnesses will doubtless win him the support of many people.

The display, vv. 8–9. Their bodies will be put on public display in the street of Jerusalem, which is identified as the city where the Lord was crucified and is characterized here as Sodom. Their bodies will be denied burial, though the Mosaic Law allowed burial the same day even for the worst of criminals (Deut. 21:22–23). This action reflects the hardened spiritual condition of the people.

> The exposure of their dead bodies tells of a most extraordinary malignity and spite, and attests the extraordinary potency and effectiveness of the objects of it. It shows at once a devilishness of unwonted intensity in the people, and a terribleness of efficiency in the Witnesses in provoking a fiendishness and resentment so monstrous and unrelenting that it could not be placated by their death, but continued to reek and vent itself upon their lifeless remains.[1]

The effect, v. 10. As if the display of their decaying bodies were not enough, the people of the earth will make a holiday of this occasion and send gifts to each other. This is the only mention of rejoicing on the earth during the entire Tribulation, and it is over the death of God's true messengers. So overjoyed are the people because their tormentors are dead that this becomes a happy holiday for them. Had they believed their witness and received their message, their deaths would have been received quite differently.

Their Translation to Heaven, 11:11–14

But God intervenes. The two witnesses will be raised up after three and a half days and be translated into heaven in "the [not 'a'] cloud [of Shekinah glory]." Their restoration to life and miraculous translation to heaven will strike fear in those who see it. Perhaps for the moment they will realize that there is a power greater than that of the Beast. It is not difficult to imagine the scene. A crowd will be standing around or filing past the decaying bodies lying in the street. Undoubtedly, there will be a great deal of radio and television coverage. Suddenly they will stand up; a voice (not the TV announcer's!) will be heard from heaven; the two witnesses, brought back to life, disappear out of sight in a cloud of glory.

The media will scarcely have time to report the story or the commentators write their columns on what happened before there will be another great event to cover: an earthquake centered in Jerusalem that destroys a tenth part of the city and kills 7,000 people. The "rest" (v. 13) does not necessarily indicate a spiritually saved group but simply those living in Jerusalem who were not killed in the earthquake. They become terrified and give glory to God. Some may be converted because of this experience, but others will simply recognize divine power without personal repentance.

This is the end of the second woe and brings the sounding of the seventh and last trumpet.

The Seventh Trumpet, 11:15–19

The Announcement of the Kingdom, 11:15

The parenthetical portion between the sixth and seventh trumpets has now concluded (10:1–11:14). This is the seventh angel's trumpet, not the trumpet of God that sounds at the Rapture of the church before the Tribulation begins (1 Thess. 4:16; cf. 1 Cor. 15:52). With the sounding of the seventh trumpet comes an announcement of the imminent rule of Christ over this world. Some additional events have to transpire before all is realized, but the end is so near now that the announcement can be made. This will bring the fulfillment of many Old Testament prophecies (Ps. 2:2; Isa. 9:6–7; Dan. 2:44).

The Adoration of God, 11:16–17

The twenty-four elders on the thrones fall down before God and worship Him for taking what is rightfully His.

The Anger of the Nations, 11:18

This verse seems to be a continuation of the words of the elders. In Christ's accomplishment of taking the reins of government, nations will be angry, the wicked dead will be punished, and the righteous will be rewarded. The anger of the nations reaches a climax in 19:19. In other words, when Christ comes to reign, full justice will be meted out and all things will be set right.

The Ark in Heaven, 11:19

That there is a temple of God in heaven is not surprising, since the tabernacle was constructed after a pattern of things in the heavens (Heb. 9:23). But the worship of God on the earth in the Tribulation temple has been defiled by the Beast. In the heavenly temple, the ark is seen at this point shining through, as it were, the lightnings, voices, thunderings, earthquake, and hail. The ark was the place of the presence of God and a reminder of the faithfulness of God. Here, just before the outpouring of final judgment, is a reminder of God's faithfulness to His own people. Things that are "opened" in the Revelation are these: a door (4:1);

the seals of the book (6:1–8:1); the Abyss (9:2); the temple in heaven (11:19); the Holy of Holies (15:5); heaven itself (19:11); and the books of works of the unsaved (20:12).

Additional Note on the Identity of the Two Witnesses

Through the years many have attempted to identify the two witnesses. This much is certain: (1) They are persons, for all the other times that the word "witness" is used in the New Testament, it is used of persons. They are not movements or powers, but two individual persons. (2) It is also clear that they are not named in the text, and I feel that the matter should be left there. They are two exceptionally empowered witnesses raised up by God during the Tribulation and protected by Him until their ministry is completed. Nevertheless, there have been many attempts at identification.

For *Elijah.* The similarity is noted between characteristics of his ministry and those of the witnesses (James 5:17; 2 Kings 1:10–12), his manner of being taken to heaven (2 Kings 2:11), and the fact that Elijah must come before the Day of the Lord (Mal. 4:5; Matt. 17:10–11).

For *Moses.* The similarity is noted between his ministry and that of the witnesses (water turned to blood, Ex. 7:20), and his presence on the Mount of Transfiguration with Elijah sets him apart as an important witness.

For *Enoch.* Since Enoch and Elijah were the only two persons to be translated without seeing death, it is argued that they will be the two witnesses, since all people must die (Heb. 9:27). But what about all those saints who will be translated in the Rapture? Also, Enoch's day was an evil one like the Tribulation.

12

WAR

12:1–17

....

Chapter 12 is a description of war—first on the earth (vv. 1–6), then in heaven (vv. 7–12), and then back on the earth (vv. 13–17). It not only reveals future things, but it also unveils the realm and activity of Satan and angels.

War On Earth—Phase 1, 12:1–6

Two Wonders, 12:1–4a

We are first introduced to two signs. "Sign" (*sēmeion*) is used seven times in the book (12:1, 3; 13:13–14; 15:1; 16:14; 19:20) to indicate an object with a special meaning.

The first sign is a "woman" (vv. 1–2). This is the second of four women mentioned in the book (the others are Jezebel, 2:20; the harlot, 17:4; the bride, 19:7). The description of this woman is reminiscent of Genesis 37:9–10. The obvious impression conveyed by the description is one of great splendor. The woman is crowned and is arrayed in great glory. The use of sun, moon, and stars is not to identify her but to describe her. Who she is must be determined from another consideration, namely, her relation to the child. Since the child is clearly Christ (from the description of His ruling in v. 5 compared with Ps. 2:9; Rev. 2:27; 19:15), the woman must be the one who bore Christ—Israel. That she is Israel and not only Mary is corroborated by the fact that it is this woman who is persecuted during the last half of the Tribulation (vv. 13–17). The woman is further described as being in travail at the birth of Christ. The picture is a paradox: a queenly woman in suffering.

The second sign is a "dragon" (vv. 3–4a). The identification of this sign is made in verse 9. The dragon is Satan, but his description in these verses is startling. The use of a dragon to picture Satan indicates his intense cruelty. The adjective "red" (v. 3) indicates his murderous, bloodthirsty character. The "seven heads and ten horns" (v. 3) relate him to the Beast (13:1), and the "diadems" (v. 3) on his heads show his authority and power. With his tail he swept away a third of the stars of heaven and "threw" (aorist tense, indicating a definite event) them to earth.

The problem is, what are the stars? They could be the luminous bodies seen in the heavens, in which case this event would be some sort of judgment involving a meteor shower on the earth. But sometimes stars refer to angelic beings (as 9:1; Job 38:7; and possibly Rev. 1:20). If that is the reference here, then the event described is the ancient revolt of Satan in which he took with him in rebellion a third of the angels (cf. Ezek. 28:15; 2 Peter 2:4; Jude 6).

The War, 12:4b–6

Verse 4b begins a separate sentence and refers back to the time of the birth of Christ and Satan's efforts to destroy Him (Matt. 2:13). Christ's birth is stated in verse 5; He is identified as the ultimate Ruler of the nations; then His ascension is mentioned, passing by His entire life and death. The reason for this omission is simply that the point of the passage is Satan's war against Christ. Satan failed to destroy Him at His birth, and the fact that He ascended proves that he failed to destroy Him during His life and even in His death. The Ascension is proof of Satan's failure and Christ's victory (Eph. 1:20–23). What is the relation of verse 6 to the story? Since Satan failed to kill Christ, he turns his attention to the woman—Israel—to pour out his vengeance on her. The details of the persecution for the last three and a half years of the Tribulation are recorded in verses 13–17.

War in Heaven, 12:7–12

The Opponents, 12:7

The scene shifts to heaven and to a war between "Michael and his angels" and "the dragon [Satan] and his angels." Michael means "Who is like God?," and he is the only angel called specifically an archangel in the Scriptures (Jude 9; cf. Dan. 10:13, 21; 12:1). Jude 9 records a conflict between the two leaders, Michael and Satan. Here the war is between them and their armies.

The Outcome, 12:8–12

In relation to the earth, vv. 8–9, 12b. The result of the battle is defeat for Satan and his army. They are cast out of heaven and onto the earth. In verse 9 Satan has five titles. "Dragon" indicates his fierce nature, "serpent" his crafty character. "Devil" means "accuser or slanderer," and "Satan" means "adversary." He is also called the one "who deceives the whole world."

In verse 12 the voice from heaven announces woe on the inhabitants of the earth because the devil has been barred from heaven and will wage his total warfare on the earth. There are two reasons for this woe in verse 12: (1) because of Satan's confinement to the earth as his only sphere of operation, and (2) because he knows he does not have much more time before his final defeat and total confinement in the Lake of Fire.

In relation to heaven, vv. 10–12a. At this defeat of Satan (which probably occurs at the middle point of the Tribulation), a voice in heaven breaks into praise. It announces salvation and the kingdom, since one more major conquest has been made in the march toward inevitable victory for Christ. Something is revealed about Satan's work through the years of history and the means of victory over him (vv. 10–11). He is labeled "the accuser of our brethren." H. A. Ironside used to say, "Satan is the accuser of the brethren; let's leave the dirty work to him!" His activity continues "day and night," and it is "before" God (thus making clear that this has been and is his work up to the middle of the Tribulation, when he will be cast from heaven).

But there is a way to have victory over Satan, and this is stated in verse 11. "They" refers to the believers of verse 10. There are three elements in the formula for victory in verse 11: (1) The basis is the blood of the Lamb. Blood is the evidence and proof of death; thus, the death of Christ is the basis for all victory over Satan. (2) The activity that overcomes Satan is testimony, or witness. Even if it leads to death (as it sometimes does), the witness will be effective in defeating Satan. (3) The attitude involved in victory is complete self-sacrifice, even to the point of being willing to die. All the inexplicable persecutions, tortures, and martyrdoms of saints in all ages are made right by this verse. Seeming defeat is ultimate victory over the enemy of our souls.

Six judgments have been or will be experienced by Satan: (1) his being put out of his original position in heaven (Ezek. 28:16); (2) the judgment pronounced by God in Eden (Gen. 3:14–15); (3) his judgment at the cross of Christ (John 12:31); (4) being cast to the earth in the middle of the Tribulation (Rev. 12:13); (5) confined to the Abyss at the beginning of the Millennium (Rev. 20:2); (6) cast into the Lake of Fire forever at the end of the Millennium (Rev. 20:10).

War on Earth—Phase 2, 12:13–17

The Antagonists, 12:13

As anticipated in verse 6, Satan's attacks after his being cast out of heaven center on the woman, Israel.

The Asylum, 12:14

Eagles' wings indicate the rapid flight that will be necessary for Israel to escape the attacks of the dragon through his agents (cf. Matt. 24:16 for the flight and Ex. 19:4; Deut. 32:11–12 for eagles' wings). Apparently these fleeing people will find asylum in some place in the wilderness that will give them a certain amount of natural protection for "a time and times and half a time," or three and one-half years (the last part of the Tribulation). Some have suggested that this wilderness refuge will be the presently deserted city of Petra in southern Palestine.

The Attack, 12:15–17

Satan (who also can cause miracles to happen) will launch his attack with a flood, apparently in an effort to flood people out of their wilderness refuge. God, in turn, will cause the earth to open (an earthquake?) in order to swallow the water of the flood and thus save the persecuted people.

When he fails to conquer or destroy those who have fled to the wilderness, Satan turns his attack on "the rest of her children." These are those who did not flee to the wilderness refuge. All those whom Satan will attack are the remnant in the sense of being on God's side; otherwise, he would not be interested in attacking them. Some flee into the wilderness asylum; the rest do not, and it is against them that Satan unleashes his attack in verse 17.

THE MIDPOINT OF THE TRIBULATION

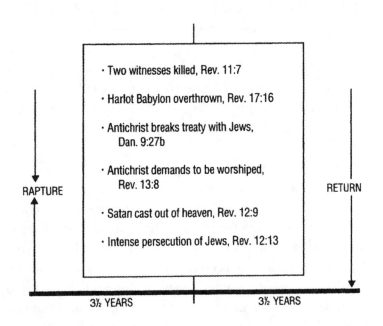

RAPTURE

RETURN

- Two witnesses killed, Rev. 11:7
- Harlot Babylon overthrown, Rev. 17:16
- Antichrist breaks treaty with Jews, Dan. 9:27b
- Antichrist demands to be worshiped, Rev. 13:8
- Satan cast out of heaven, Rev. 12:9
- Intense persecution of Jews, Rev. 12:13

3½ YEARS   3½ YEARS

THE BEAST AND HIS FALSE PROPHET

13:1–18

....

The First Beast, 13:1–10

His Appearance, 13:1–2

This Beast has already been introduced in 11:7, but now his person and work are described more completely. Though there have been many antichrists throughout church history, this is the great and final Antichrist who is still to come (1 John 2:18). In this vision he arose "out of the sea," which many understand to be a symbol of the masses of people (17:15). But perhaps his origin out of the sea simply distinguishes him in the vision from the second beast, who arises out of the land. The Beast has seven heads, ten horns, crowns on the horns, and the names of blasphemy on his heads. The Beast heads a kingdom, for the ten horns are identified as ten kings in 17:12, yet they are united in one Beast. In other words, he represents a confederation of ten nations. The seven heads are also explained in 17:9 as the seven hills of the city in which his power centers (Rome). They also stand for seven Roman rulers, of which he is the last.

Therefore, the Beast is not only a kingdom but also an individual ruler. He is a man. This is known from 2 Thessalonians 2:3–4 and Matthew 24:15, where he as an individual—not a kingdom—sits in the temple as God. That is why his heads are covered with "words [the plural is correct] and blasphemies." Roman emperors in the past blasphemed by designating themselves as God. This man will do the same.

In total appearance the Beast was *"like* a leopard," his feet *"like* those of a bear," and his mouth *like* a lion's. In the vision of Daniel 7 the first beast that the prophet saw was like a lion, the second like a bear, and the third like a leopard. John's Beast combines these features; whatever the Babylonian, Medo-Persian, and Grecian empires had of strength, brutality, and swiftness will be present in this final form of Antichrist's world rule in the Western confederation of nations (or, as it is sometimes called, the revived Roman Empire).

Great as this man and empire will be, he is actually only an agent or tool of someone else. It is the dragon, Satan, who gives the Beast his power, throne, and authority. He is sold out to Satan, and Satan uses him to the maximum.

His Acclaim, 13:3-4

The cause of it, v. 3. One of the heads of the Beast was (literally) "as having been slain to death." This is exactly the same word that was used in 5:6 of the Lamb, where it is translated "as if slain." Since Christ died actually, it appears that Antichrist will also actually die. But his wound will be healed, which can only mean restoration to life. In 11:7 he was seen as coming out of the Abyss, and that coincides with his restoration to life here. He apparently actually dies, descends to the Abyss, and returns to life on earth. No wonder the world will acclaim him.

The character of it, v. 4. The world will worship the Beast. The "whole earth" of verse 3 is qualified by verse 8. Those whose names are written in the Book of Life will not worship him, but all others will. Worship means acknowledgment of worth, and the worth people acknowledge in the Beast is twofold: his uniqueness ("Who is like the beast?") and his might ("Who is able to wage war with him?").

His Activities, 13:5–7a

His activities include blasphemy and war. Notice that the former is a religious activity and the latter a political one. He is not only a political ruler, but he seeks to exert religious domination too. His mouth speaks great things and blasphemies against God (cf. Dan. 7:25). He will blaspheme the name of God, the dwelling place of God (His tabernacle), and those who dwell in heaven (the saints who will already be there).

Further, the Beast will be allowed ("it was given," v. 7) to make war with the saints (cf. 12:17). "Overcome" indicates that he will kill them. All of this activity, however, is directly under the control of God. His ability to make war is permitted by God, and all his power is limited to forty-two months (v. 5). Here is an example of the interweaving of the forces that go to make up events: God controls all, yet Satan controls the Beast, who, in turn, acts on his own in blaspheming. Those who compose his army will serve him and make martyrs of God's people, who, though they give up their lives, are still within God's protecting care!

His Authority, 13:7b–10

The extent of it, vv. 7b–8. The Beast's authority extends to all peoples except those whose names are in the Book of Life. The phrase "book of life" occurs seven times in Revelation (3:5; 13:8;

17:8; 20:12, 15; 21:27; 22:19) and only one time elsewhere in the New Testament (Phil. 4:3).

The end of it, vv. 9–10. Verse 9 is a call to serious attention. An important principle is about to be announced in verse 10. It is the principle of retribution. After all that has been said about the power of the Beast, verse 10 contains a word of great comfort. The captor will be taken captive; the killer will be killed. When God's purposes are finished through Antichrist, God will take him captive and confine him to the Lake of Fire. Knowing this brings the patience and faith that sustains the saints who endure these persecutions.

The False Prophet, 13:11–18

His Appearance, 13:11

This second beast arises from the earth and is thereby distinguished from the first one, who came from the sea in the vision. His appearance also is different—less pretentious. He has two horns (instead of ten) like a lamb. The horns suggest strength, though less strength than the first Beast, and the lamb may allude to an appearance of meekness or innocence and may also indicate his character as an imitation of the Lamb of God. This beast is no weak person, however, for he speaks as a dragon.

His Aim, 13:12

The aim of this second person is to promote the worship of the first Beast. At no time in his career does he promote himself, but his interests are always concerned with those of the first Beast. Verse 12 declares that his power is as great as that of the first Beast, but he uses it in the interests of the first Beast.

His Activity, 13:13–17

In order to accomplish his aim, this second beast will be empowered to do certain things.

Fire on earth. He will make fire come down on the earth in imitation of the power of the two witnesses, to show the world that he has as much power as they had (v. 13).

Other miracles. He will perform other miracles (vv. 13–14).

Image of first Beast. He will order those on the earth to make an image of the first Beast (v. 14), and from what follows it appears that they will do it willingly and quickly, for his next step is to give breath to the image they make. The word for breath is *pneuma* ("spirit"). This could indicate a supernatural miracle (performed by the power of Satan) that actually gives life to the image. Or the word may be translated "wind" and indicate some technological feat performed by the second beast that gives the appearance of real life and speech to this image. However, since it is the image that causes those who do not worship it to be killed, this may indicate that it has actual life.

Identification with the Beast. He will force people to become identified with the Beast by a mark that they must receive on their foreheads or right hands. The word "mark" means "an impress made by a stamp," like a brand used on slaves and animals. People will become slaves of the Beast and have the identifying mark of their slavery. Without it they cannot buy or sell.

What will this mark be like? Verse 17 indicates that it will be either the name of the Beast or the number of his name. Greek letters also stand for numbers. The number is further explained in verse 18 as 666. Evidently, people will be stamped with the number 666 or the name for which those numbers stand. In that coming day this will also be a means of identifying the Beast to those who constitute the godly remnant.

Many characters in history have been identified with the number 666, but all are mistaken. When this man arises on the scene of world affairs, there will be no mistake as to who he is, and in some way, unknown now, the number 666 will play a principal part in the identification. The mark is of the first Beast, however, for he is the chief character in this chapter and the one whose worship is promoted by the second beast. For this reason, the second beast is called elsewhere the False Prophet of the first Beast (16:13; 19:20; 20:10).

Additional Note on the Title "Antichrist"

The term "antichrist" is a biblical one (1 John 2:18, 22; 4:3; 2 John 7). It is used both of false teachers in John's day (and by example it may be used of false teachers in any day) and of the coming Antichrist. In other words, the word is properly used in both the present and future and in both the singular and plural.

Which of these beasts is the Antichrist? The meaning of the word will not determine the answer, for both beasts are antichrists in the sense of being against Christ. Some feel that the second beast is the Antichrist because he has to do chiefly with religious matters, while the first Beast is principally concerned with polit-ical activities. But the first Beast is clearly a religious leader too, for he demands to be worshiped. Sometimes Daniel 11:37 is cited as showing that the Antichrist will be a Jew, and the reference is linked with the fact that the second beast comes from the land (symbolizing Israel). However, Daniel 11:37 might be translated "gods" as well as "God." It seems to me that the label "Antichrist" is to be used with the more important personage, and that, of course, is the first Beast. First John 2:18 indicates that there is coming one great Antichrist. The Lord predicted that there would be many false prophets and many who claim to be Christ during the tribulation days (Matt. 24:11, 23–24). The title "Antichrist," therefore, ought to be applied to the outstanding person among all these false people, and that is the first Beast. Also, the first Beast is the man of sin (2 Thess. 2:3), the little horn (Dan. 7:8), the prince that shall come (Dan. 9:26), the king who does as he pleases (Dan. 11:36), and the Beast (Rev. 11:7; 13:1–2; 14:9, 11; 16:2, 10, 13; 17:3, 17; 19:19–20; 20:4, 10).

VARIOUS
ANNOUNCEMENTS

14:1–20

....

The 144,000, 14:1–5

Their Situation, 14:1

The vision opens with John seeing the Lamb and 144,000 on Mount Zion. Some understand this to be anticipatory of the millennial state, making Zion mean the earthly Jerusalem as it sometimes does (2 Sam. 5:7; Isa. 2:3). But since Zion is used of the heavenly Jerusalem (Heb. 12:22) and since these 144,000 are before the throne (v. 3), it seems more natural to understand Zion as the heavenly city. The important point, however, is that the 144,000 are now with the Lamb. When the group was first introduced they were on earth (7:1–3), but now they are in heaven. Their work of witnessing must now be finished, for none will be able to slay them until then. That they are the same group as in chapter 7 seems clear because (1) the distinctive number is exactly the same, and (2) God's name is written on their foreheads.

Their Song, 14:2–3

John next heard a great sound like "the sound of many waters" and "the sound of loud thunder" (v. 2). It resolved itself into "the sound of harpists" (v. 2) playing on harps and singing a new song. Verse 2 apparently speaks of the same group as verse 3, that is, the 144,000. Notice too that the 144,000 are distinct from the elders and the living ones.

Their Separation, 14:4a, b

Two things are said about their separation unto God. First, they are virgins. Although this could be understood to mean that these people were never married and therefore undistracted in their work for God (as in 1 Cor. 7:32), it also can mean that they were completely separated unto the God they served. The word "virgin" is used this way of married Corinthian believers in 2 Corinthians 11:2. It includes men in that passage, in Matthew 25:1, and here. Second, they follow Christ "wherever He goes," including unto death.

Their Salvation, 14:4c

They are redeemed people ("purchased") and "first fruits." From the Old Testament use of "first fruits," this means that they are a token offering to God, which indicates that a larger harvest will follow. The first converts of a country are called first fruits of the larger number to be won (Rom. 16:5; 1 Cor. 16:15). Christ is the first fruits of the resurrection harvest (1 Cor. 15:20, 23). Of what group are these 144,000 the first fruits? Apparently they indicate the harvest of many other Israelites (remember that they are Jews, not Gentiles) who will turn to the Lord at the end of the Tribulation and during the Millennium (Isa. 2:3; Zech. 8:22; 12:10; Rom. 11:25).

Their Sanctification, 14:5

Their mouths spoke no lies (that is, no false messages) but only the truth about Christ as the only way to heaven. They were blameless or unblemished (that is, true teachers in contrast to false teachers, who are labeled "blemishes" in 2 Peter 2:13).

The Everlasting Gospel, 14:6–7

Its Announcement, 14:6

An angel appears with the announcement of an everlasting gospel. (See Gal. 1:8, though God does not use angels today to proclaim the gospel.) The content certainly includes the meaning that the death of Christ is key to bringing everlasting life to those who believe.

Its Inclusiveness, 14:6

The message of this gospel is to all the world. It is God's last call of grace to a world that persists in rejecting Him and that openly defies Him.

Its Message, 14:7

Its message is threefold: fear, glorify, and worship God, who is about to judge the world. The particular aspect of God's revelation of Himself in this message is as *Creator*. If people heed this message, they will have to refuse to receive the mark of the Beast, which will show as clearly as possible a heart change. In those days people will not risk their lives at the hands of the Beast for a mere outward profession of salvation.

The Doom of Babylon, 14:8

The rest of this chapter is something like a table of contents for the remainder of the book. Another angel now announces the fall of Babylon, which is described in detail in chapters 17 and 18.

Its Certainty

The repetition of "fallen" emphasizes the certainty of the complete destruction of Babylon. This is anticipatory, since Babylon's actual fall is connected with the outpouring of the seventh bowl (16:19).

Its Cause

The reason for Babylon's judgment is twofold: because of her own immorality, and because she has infected all the nations with her sins.

The Doom of Beast Worshipers, 14:9–13

The People Doomed, 14:9

The third angel announces judgment on all who worship the Beast and his image and who receive his mark. Notice that the mark may be placed on the forehead where all can see or in the hand where it could be hidden temporarily.

Their Punishment, 14:10–11

The punishment is described in terrible terms that occur elsewhere in the Bible. Its intensity is unmixed—literally, "he shall drink of the wine of the anger of God mixed undiluted in the cup of his wrath." Its agents are "fire and brimstone," or sulphur. It will be a spectacle "in the presence of the holy angels" and "the Lamb," whom these people rejected. Throughout eternity, the Lake of Fire is in the presence of the Lord, for nothing can be outside His omnipresence, even the Lake of Fire. However, the wicked will be separated from His presence in the sense of contact and fellowship (see 2 Thess. 1:9, where a different preposition is used). Its extent is forever (v. 11). Its character is continuous ("no rest day and night," v. 11).

The Perseverance of the Saints, 14:12–13

In spite of the intensity of Antichrist's endeavors to bring all the world under his control, there will be some who will not yield but who will keep the commandments of God. In the midst of their persecution by the Beast, they will be helped to endure by remembering that ultimately the Beast and all his followers will have to suffer the eternal punishment described in verses 10–11. This verse is similar to 13:10b.

A further announcement is made concerning those whom the Beast will martyr in verse 13. They are called "blessed." "From now on" indicates that this blessing belongs particularly to those who will suffer under the Beast. Their works in standing for the truth follow them into heaven.

The Harvest of the Earth, 14:14–20

The Reapers, 14:14–18

The reapers of the harvest are the Lord (vv. 14, 16) and angels (v. 17). The Lord is pictured with "a golden crown" (*stephanos,* a victor's crown, not a diadem, indicating His coming as Conqueror) and "a sharp sickle" (to do the work of judging). An angel (v. 15) from the temple delivers the command from God to proceed with the harvest, and another angel (v. 17), also from the presence of God, appears with a sharp sickle to help in the harvesting (cf. Matt. 13:39).

The Reason, 14:15, 18

Within this section two figures are used: the harvest (vv. 14–16) and the vine (vv. 17–19). The harvest is said to be ripe (v. 15) and the grapes of the vine are also said to be ripe (v. 18). The two words are different, however. The ripe harvest in verse 15 depicts a dried or withered harvest (cf. Matt. 21:19–20; Mark 3:1, 3; John 15:6; Rev. 16:12). In other words, the inhabitants of the earth are withered, lifeless, and fully ready for judgment. The grapes on the vine in verse 18 are also said to be ripe; that is, full of juice and ready to burst. This is the vine of the earth and stands in contrast to Christ, the true vine (Ps. 80:8; John 15:1). The picture here is that all false human religions are fully ripe and ready for harvest. Thus, the harvest is ready because humankind in its own efforts, apart from the life of God, has fully developed an apostate religious system.

The Result, 14:19–20

If verses 14–16 picture the harvest of Matthew 13:36–43, then, of course, there will be some who will be taken into kingdom blessing while others go into judgment. But the harvest of the grapes results only in judgment in the winepress of the wrath of God. In verse 20 this judgment is specified not as hell but as something that occurs on the earth, the city being Jerusalem. It apparently is a reference to the war of Armageddon (cf. 19:17–19) when the blood from the slaughter will flow 1,600 furlongs, or 180 miles, to the depth of the horses' bridles (or about four and a half feet). If at the end of the Tribulation, 1.5 to 2 billion people remain on the earth, and if 10 percent of them are fighting at Armageddon, that means 150 to 200 million people will be fighting and, presumably, most slaughtered. The valley of Megiddo, where the war will be fought in the north of Palestine, drains into the Jordan Valley and Dead Sea, allowing sufficient distance to literally fulfill this prediction.

PRELUDE TO THE LAST JUDGMENTS

15:1–8

....

The Plagues, 15:1

As with the trumpet judgments, angels are employed in the execution of these seven last plagues. When they have been poured out on the earth, then the "wrath" (literally, "anger") of God is finished. That means that His wrath began sometime before these judgments; therefore, the church, which is promised deliverance from the wrath, could not be raptured at the close of the Tribulation as posttribulationism teaches. When the seventh bowl is poured out, a voice again cries, "It is done" (16:17).

The People, 15:2–4

Their Identity, 15:2

John saw as it were "a sea of glass mixed with fire." Such a sea appeared in the vision in 4:6 but here is mingled with fire, perhaps referring to the fiery persecution these people had suffered under the Beast. The group is clearly identified as those who achieved victory over the Beast, even though it cost them their lives. Undoubtedly the Beast will think himself victorious over his enemies, whom he kills, but God says that they get victory over him (cf. 12:11). They have "harps" like the twenty-four elders (5:8) and the 144,000 (14:3). These martyrs are in heaven, not in purgatory, and they are singing (15:3), an activity that would be impossible if their souls were asleep between physical death and resurrection (cf. also 6:9–11).

Their Activity, 15:3–4

They sing the song of Moses and the Lamb, ascribing praise to God for His mighty acts (cf. Ex. 15 and Deut. 32). The word "song" is repeated before the phrase "of the Lamb," indicating that they sing two songs: the song of Moses and the song of the Lamb (could this be Psalm 22?). The substance of both songs is the mighty works of God. To Him are ascribed several things: (1) He is almighty (cf. 1:8); (2) He is righteous and true. This attribute is particularly relevant in relation to the outpouring of these judgments; (3) He is the King of the "nations" (not "saints," as in the KJV). This kingship is about to be exercised, for the setting up of the kingdom on the earth is imminent; (4) He is holy, and for this reason people should fear and glorify Him (cf. 14:7); and (5) He will be worshiped by the nations, again referring to the time of the establishment of the kingdom. This is the One whose wrath is about to be poured out in these seven last plagues.

The Preparation, 15:5–8

A new vision opens that involves the commissioning of the outpouring of these plagues. It is a vision of the temple in heaven and particularly of the "tabernacle of the testimony"— that is, the Holy of Holies. It is opened to reveal seven angels coming out. This emphasizes that the judgments of God demonstrate and vindicate His holiness since they come out of the sanctuary itself.

To these angels comes one of the four living ones with "seven golden bowls" of these last judgments. The word "bowls" (not "vials," as in the KJV) depicts something like an incense bowl (cf. 5:8 for the same word). These bowls contain the wrath, or anger, of God, and until they are poured out no one can enter the temple because of the "smoke" (probably a symbol of the judgment connected with these plagues, as in Ex. 19:18; Isa. 6:4). Certainly the smoke adds to the total picture of the terror of these imminent judgments.

ARMAGEDDON

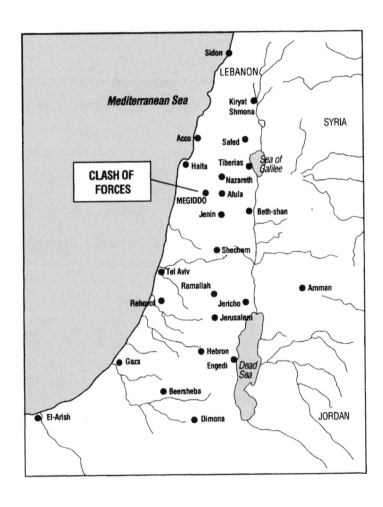

THE SEVEN BOWL JUDGMENTS

16:1–21

....

Unlike the previous series of judgments of the trumpets and seals, each of which had a break between the sixth and seventh judgments, the seven plagues of the bowls are poured out without interruption and apparently quite rapidly. All the angels receive their orders to go at the same time (v. 1), which would indicate that these judgments follow each other in quick succession.

The First Bowl, 16:2

The first plague comes upon the earth and results in a "loathsome and malignant sore" inflicted on people. Swete believes this means malignant in a medical sense.[1] The group afflicted is limited to those who are followers of Antichrist, the believing remnant being exempt (cf. Ex. 9:8–12). Apparently the Beast cannot heal them, for they are still cursing God for these sores after the fifth bowl has been poured out (v. 11). Notice too that the Beast is in power and that his image has been set up and worshiped when this first bowl judgment comes. Therefore, this series of judgments will occur at the close of the tribulation period.

The Second Bowl, 16:3

When the second bowl is poured on the sea, it results in the waters becoming like the blood of a dead man and "every living thing in the sea" dying. The illustration vividly depicts a dying person wallowing in his own blood. In like manner, the seas will wallow in blood. Under the second trumpet, one-third of the sea creatures died (8:9); now the destruction is complete. The stench and disease this will bring, especially along the shores of the seas of the earth, are unimaginable.

The Third Bowl, 16:4–7

The third plague follows the pattern of the third trumpet and makes the fresh water supply become blood. The victims of this judgment will experience the relentless law of retribution. They shed the blood of the saints and prophets, so they must now drink blood. Apparently this bloody water is not toxic and can be drunk. "They deserve it" (v. 6) refers to the victims of this judgment. They deserve what they receive. Another angel from the altar echoes the refrain of the righteousness of God's judgments. The only reason it is difficult for people to conceive of God dealing in this manner is that for thousands of years He has been long-suffering and gracious, not meting out the judgment the world deserved.

The Fourth Bowl, 16:8–9

The fourth judgment affects the sun so that power "was given to it to scorch" people. That the Day of the Lord would come like a burning furnace was predicted in Malachi 4:1. Instead of turning to God and pleading for mercy, people blaspheme His name and do not repent.

The fallout from this judgment staggers the imagination. Henry Morris writes,

The intense solar radiation will again evaporate great quantities of water from the oceans and other water surfaces, lowering sea level and water tables. . . . Thus, more and more water vapor will remain aloft. . . . Rain and hail as do reach the surface [of the earth] will probably be in the form of violent thunderstorm and tornado cells, adding yet more to earth's misery. . . .

However, the intense heat of the sun will also produce another effect which will, at least for a time, somewhat compensate for oceanic evaporation. That is, the great ice sheets on Greenland and the continent of Antarctica will melt. There is enough ice stored in these great reservoirs, it is estimated, to raise the world's sea levels about 200 feet if it were all melted. . . .

If, indeed, the great ice caps should suddenly melt one day, many of the world's greatest cities would be largely inundated and destroyed.[2]

The Fifth Bowl, 16:10–11

The fifth plague comes on the "throne" of the Beast and brings darkness to the seat of his government. Undoubtedly, this slows up his attempt to force all people to worship him or be killed. Apparently Antichrist will not have enough time then to be able to enforce his edict on all the world. The result of this plague is that people gnaw their tongues and blaspheme God for their pains and sores (which they received under the previous judgments and which are still with them).

The Sixth Bowl, 16:12–16

The sixth judgment will dry up the Euphrates River (which previously had been turned to blood). This is done to facilitate the crossing of the armies of "the kings from the east" (cf. Dan. 11:44) as they march to the final war of Armageddon. This is an actual drying up of the river that forms the eastern border of Palestine (Gen. 15:18).

The mention of the kings of the East introduces an excursus on Armageddon (vv. 13–16). John saw "three unclean spirits like frogs" come out of the mouths of the trinity of evil—the dragon (Satan), the Beast (13:1–10), and the False Prophet (13:11–18). They are identified as "demons" (v. 14), and their task is to bring the kings of the earth to the war of Armageddon ("Har-Magedon"). This word means "hill of Megiddo," which is located on the southern rim of the plain of Esdraelon. That is where the war (series of battles) will take place. God is directing this (v. 19); demons accomplish it by using earthly rulers (v. 16); Satan, the Beast, and the False Prophet are involved in it (v. 13); yet the kings of the earth will think they are making decisions of their own free will (Dan. 11:44). How intricate are the ways of God!

In the midst of this statement about Armageddon comes a warning and an appeal for purity and watchfulness (v. 15). Grace is still offered even in the face of persistent and shameless rejection.

The Seventh Bowl, 16:17–21

The last judgment brings widespread destruction and havoc. With it comes the cry, "It is done." This is accompanied by physical signs and disturbances. The earthquake divides "the great city"—Jerusalem (cf. Zech. 14:4, 8)—and causes other cities to fall. Babylon is fully judged (details are in chaps. 17–18), islands and mountains disappear, and a great hailstorm occurs, each hailstone weighing about 100 pounds.

Yet, in spite of the severity and universality of these last judgments, some people will survive and—unbelievable as it is—will persist in blaspheming God rather than turning to Him for mercy. Everything that humanity has built will crumble before their eyes.

Quite literally the whole world will collapse around them, yet they will persist in thinking that they are still masters of their own fate, without any need for God.

The conclusion of this series of judgments brings us to the second coming of Christ. This is described in chapter 19, but John is first given a vision of the details concerning Babylon, which has been mentioned several times before.

RELIGIOUS BABYLON

17:1–18

....

Babylon has had a long and consistently dishonorable history. It had its beginnings around 3000 BC under Nimrod (Gen. 10:8–10). The tower of Babel (Gen. 11:1–9) was built to prevent people from scattering throughout the earth, in direct defiance of God's command to do so. Hammurabi made Babylon a religious power about 1600 BC by making Marduk god of the city of Babylon and head of a pantheon of 1,300 deities. Extrabiblical sources indicate that the wife of Nimrod became the head of the Babylonian mysteries, which consisted of religious rites that were part of the worship of idols in Babylon. Her name was Semiramis, and she supposedly gave birth to a son, Tammuz, who claimed to be a savior and the fulfillment of the promise given to Eve in Genesis 3:15.

This anti-God Babylonian religion is alluded to in Ezekiel 8:14, Jeremiah 7:18, and 44:17–19, 25. The queen of heaven in these passages is the goddess Ishtar, an Assyro-Babylonian deity. The fourth Babylonian month, July, was named Tammuz.

The zenith of Babylonia's glory came during the reign of Nebuchadnezzar (604–562 BC; cf. Dan. 4:30). But in 539 Babylon was captured by Darius the Mede, and the city began to decline.

From about 300 BC the city has been in decay. However, in 1986 Saddam Hussein, portraying himself as the successor to Nebu-chadnezzar, began to rebuild Babylon, which lies about fifty miles south of Baghdad in Iraq.

Many understand the prophecies of Jeremiah 50–51 to teach that Babylon will never be rebuilt. Others feel that it will be rebuilt, at least in the region of ancient Babylon. The symbolic removing of evil from Israel to Babylon in Zechariah 5:11 may support the rebuilding of Babylon on the Euphrates as a center of the eschatological Babylon. The present activity in that area does not yet qualify as a rebuilding of Babylon, though this could change in the future, and Babylon on the Euphrates in present-day Iraq might become the capital, or a capital, of the system detailed in Revelation 17–18.

However, still others, on the basis of 1 Peter 5:13, understand Babylon to be a cryptic reference to Rome. If so, Peter is describing under the label "Babylon" the spiritual nature of Rome, the city, the empire, the civilization, as anti-God. This might indicate that Rome will be the capital, or a capital, of the Babylonian system of Revelation 17–18.

The destruction of Babylon, which has already been referred to in the book (14:8; 16:19), is now described in detail in chapters 17 and 18. The emphasis in chapter 17 is on the religious and political aspects of Babylon and in chapter 18 on the commercial system. Babylon is both a city and a system, and that seems to be the way it is used in these chapters. This is much the same way Americans speak of Wall Street or Madison Avenue. They are actual streets, but they also stand for the financial or advertising enterprises. Babylon is used in a similar sense in these chapters, standing for a religious and political system in chapter 17 and a commercial empire in chapter 18.

The Description Of Babylon, 17:1–7

It was one of the bowl angels who revealed these details to John. The words "Come here" occur again in 21:9.

Some Details, 17:1–6

She is a harlot, vv. 1–2. Four times this false religious system of the Tribulation is characterized as a harlot because she is unfaithful to the Lord (vv. 1, 5, 15–16; cf. 19:2). Furthermore, she is labeled "the great harlot" (v. 1), indicating that she represents the epitome of unfaithfulness. Also, "she sits on many waters," indicating that her system will stretch around the world (though not to the exclusion of the existence of other religions at that time). When believers are taken to heaven in the Rapture before the Tribulation begins, religion does not disappear from the earth. Indeed, it will flourish under this unfaithful Babylon for the first half of the Tribulation, until destroyed by the Beast.

Babylon will likely build on the remnants of the professing Christian church that existed before the Rapture. Professing Christians who will not be raptured will remain to form the base of this "church." Tribulation saints, of course, will oppose this false church. The harlotry of this system will extend to "many waters," which means to many people (v. 15) and will include alliances with leaders of the earth. In other words, the power of this church will be enhanced by political alliances.

She has great political power, v. 3. John next saw the woman sitting on the Beast. The Beast is clearly seen to be the man of sin of 13:1–10 by comparing the description in verse 3 with 13:1. The startling feature of this scene is that the whore is sitting on the Beast, indicating that she will have power over the man of sin. This event must occur during the first part of the Tribulation before the man of sin overthrows religion and requires everyone to worship him.

She displays magnificent glory, v. 4. The harlot is bedecked with splendor, signifying the glory and wealth with which she will entice people. Even amid the awful judgments of the first part of the Tribulation this false "church" will try to take people's minds off what is happening and allure them with false comfort.

She is in reality a counterfeit, v. 5a. Her name is called "a mystery." (Note that the word "mystery" is not an adjective—"mystery Babylon"—but a noun in apposition to Babylon—"mystery, Babylon.") The Christian will realize by the use of this word "mystery" that this Babylon is not the city on the Euphrates but a secret use of the word (explained in 17:9, 18). Since the true church is also called a mystery (Eph. 5:32), this apostate church is a counterfeit.

She may be organized as a federation, 5b. The harlot is also the "mother of harlots." The mother harlot has a family of harlots. In other words, many groups will join together under the one harlot in a kind of federated church. She will incorporate various denominations and religious groups without necessarily amalgamating them. If this is the way the organization will be formed, then the various groups within it can keep their doctrinal and polity distinctives and still unite in this harlot family relationship.

She persecutes the saints, v. 6. Babylon will be a persecutor of the believers in Jesus during this time, and she will be successful in doing that.

A Promise to John, 17:7

The entire vision seems to have been enigmatic to John. The angel asks him, "Why do you wonder?" Then the angel promises John an explanation of the matters he had seen.

Interpretation of the Description of Babylon, 17:8–15

The Beast, 17:8

The Beast is identified first. He is the same one referred to in 11:7 as coming from the Abyss. Here it is said that he "is about to come up," indicating that the events of verses 1–7 precede his seizure of power in the middle of the tribulation period.

The Seven Heads, 17:9–11

The seven heads of the Beast are identified as the "seven mountains on which the woman [harlot] sits." "No reasonable doubt can be entertained as to the meaning of these words. The seven hills of Rome were a commonplace with the Latin poets."[1] This is true even though Rome is actually built on more than seven hills. In other words, the center of the harlot church's power will be Rome.

As to the identification of the "seven kings" (v. 10), there is greater difficulty. They apparently have something to do with Rome, and some have interpreted them as a selective list of Roman emperors (since more than five had reigned up to John's time). Others have suggested that they refer to a selective list of world empires up to that time. Questions can be raised to both of these views, and the matter cannot be settled with certainty. In any case, the Beast that is to come during the Tribulation is definitely said to be the "eighth" in whatever list is meant (v. 11), and his power is limited by God and his doom certain.

The Ten Horns, 17:12–14

The horns of the Beast are ten kings (Dan. 7:23–24). These are the ten Western nations headed by Antichrist who are allowed to rule for "one hour." That expression should be understood as meaning "one purpose or activity" (cf. Luke 22:53). To suit the

Beast's own purpose they are allowed to rule as seemingly independent entities. But this independence is only on the surface. They will give their power to the Beast (v. 13) and together make war with the Lamb. Daniel reveals that three of these ten nations will evidently rebel so that the Beast has to take them over forcibly (7:24). Of course, they cannot defeat the Lamb, so they are overcome. Christ's titles, "King of kings" and "Lord of lords," are especially significant in light of the lordship the Beast will assume over these kings.

The Waters, 17:15

The waters on which the harlot sits (v. 1) are now explained as the peoples of the world. The apostate church will be ecumenical (which means worldwide).

The Destruction of Babylon, 17:16–18

Religious Babylon, which sought political alliances and power, will in the end be destroyed by a political alliance. It will be these ten nations who "make her desolate." The words "desolate," "naked," "eat," and "burn" all show the completeness of her annihilation.

In verse 17 we find another example of the interweaving of the purposes of God with the desires of people. The kings will voluntarily join forces to destroy the harlot, but in so doing they are, in reality, fulfilling the purpose of God. It is God who will incline them to align themselves with the Beast until, literally, "the words of God are finished or accomplished."

Finally, the identification of the woman is further linked to the great city previously mentioned (v. 9), that is, Rome. This makes it impossible to disassociate apostate Christendom of the tribulation days from Rome. Rome will evidently be both the religious and political center of the world in the Tribulation.

To summarize this chapter: religion will flourish during the first part of the Tribulation in the false system called Babylon, the harlot. This system likely centers in the city of Rome, includes other harlot groups, and exercises great political influence. For the first half of the Tribulation, the harlot will reign unchallenged; but at the middle of the Tribulation, the Beast (the man of sin, Antichrist) will see her as a challenge to his own power and program. So with his league of ten nations he will destroy the harlot and set himself up as God, demanding to be worshiped.

COMMERCIAL BABYLON

18:1–24

....

Babylon involves a city (evidently Rome and perhaps Babylon on the Euphrates) and a system. The religious aspect of that system was described in the preceding chapter; this chapter concerns other facets of Babylon, chiefly commercial ones (vv. 3, 7, 9, 11–13, 19). In addition, there is another difference between these two chapters. In chapter 17 it was the Beast and his allies who destroyed the harlot Babylon. Here it is God who destroys this other aspect of Babylon (v. 8).

The Announcement of the Judgment, 18:1–3

The agent of the announcement is another angel who has great power (v. 1). There is no need to identify this being as Christ since angels do have great power. He illumines the earth with his glory, apparently reversing for a time the darkness that came as part of the fifth bowl judgment (16:10). In his cry concerning the falling of Babylon, he repeats for emphasis "fallen." He also reveals some facts about Babylon that show how evil the system is and how righteous God is in destroying it.

Babylon is demonic (v. 2). This is emphasized in three phrases. It is the "dwelling place of demons," the "prison of every unclean spirit" (cf. Eph. 2:2; 1 John 4:6, where demons are called spirits), and the "prison of every unclean and hateful bird." This latter phrase possibly alludes to the birds in the parable of the mustard seed (Matt. 13:31–32), indicating the demonic forces at work in the apostate system.

Babylon is unfaithful (v. 3). This charge of fornication, or unfaithfulness to the Lord, is repeated here as in the previous chapter.

Babylon is intoxicating (v. 3). All nations drink of the wine of her unfaithfulness, and "merchants" particularly have succumbed to her luxuries and become satisfied with their ill-gained riches. The system rewards her votaries with careless ease, and they are satisfied. No wonder they weep over her destruction.

The Appeal in View of the Judgment, 18:4–8

The Statement of the Appeal, 18:4

The call is for God's people to come out of Babylon and not partake of her sins, so that they may escape her judgments. In its primary interpretation, this appeal will be addressed to Tribulation believers who, like believers in every age, will be tempted to compromise. In its application, it is a relevant call to believers of all time periods to avoid compromise with Satan's world system in its every form—religious and commercial. See Genesis 19:12–14; Numbers 16:23–26; Isaiah 48:20; 2 Corinthians 6:14–17; 1 John 2:15–17 for more on the world's system.

The Substantiation for the Appeal, 18:5–8

The appeal for separation is substantiated on the basis of three inescapable truisms.

Remembrance, v. 5. The first Babel confederacy tried to build a tower to heaven (Gen. 11:4); the last piles up her sins to heaven, and God remembers. Although He acts with such longsuffering that people may think He does not notice what is happening, God remembers; and because of this, the judgment of Babylon is inevitable and just.

Retribution, v. 6. In the case of Babylon, retributive judgment is doubled in severity because of the enormity of her sins.

Retaliation, vv. 7–8. In place of the glory and luxury with which she has clothed herself, God retaliates with torment and sorrow. The verb that means "lived sensuously" is the same root as the noun in verse 3. In place of her assumed position as queen with many lovers ("not a widow"), God gives plagues, death, mourning, and famine. Her lovers are the kings of the earth (17:2; 18:3), but in reality she is a widow because of forsaking the Lord.

There is no reason not to understand her final destruction as coming "in one day" (v. 8). It happened before with another Babylon (Dan. 5:1, 3–5, 30), and it often occurs with individuals (Luke 12:19–20). The burning, too, is to be understood plainly and evidently refers to the burning of the city or cities that are the center of Babylon in its several forms. Christians were once burned because they were accused of having burned Rome. God will burn that city, among others, in His judgment on this day.

The Anguish Because of the Judgment on Babylon, 18:9–19

By Kings, 18:9–10

The first lament is from the "kings of the earth." They "weep and lament" when they see the smoke of the fire. Notice that they stand at a distance trying to avoid doom on themselves, but in reality they only postpone it. Again, the suddenness and swiftness of the judgment is emphasized in the phrase "one hour."

By Merchants, 18:11–17a

The "merchants of the earth weep and mourn," for they see the source of their careless ease vanishing before their eyes. This motive for their lamentation is plainly stated in verse 11b. It is not that they care about Babylon, but they do care about their businesses. Their merchandise is varied and includes costly ornaments (gold, silver, precious stones, pearls, 12a); expensive clothes (fine linen, purple, silk, scarlet, 12b); rich furnishings (citron wood—a kind of cypress—articles of ivory, costly wood, bronze, iron, and marble, 12c); precious perfumes (cinnamon, spice, incense, frankincense, 13a); foods (wine, oil, fine flour, wheat, cattle, sheep, 13b); conveyances (horses, chariots, 13c); and even human chattel (slaves—literally, bodies and souls of humans, 13d).

Two features should be noted about this list: first, most of the items are luxury items, and, second, apparently these merchants will be trafficking in people as well as things. The depth of their sin is covered with the veneer of their luxurious and contented living. All this goes on in the midst of the terrible judgments of the Tribulation.

But in a certain hour of a certain day this will end, and in the midst of the destruction the merchants will stand far off, weeping and sorrowing. They stand "at a distance" because of the "fear of her torment" (v. 15), and their lament is centered in the fact that their great riches have come to nothing in so short a time (vv. 17–18). There will be a stock market crash and bankruptcy on a worldwide scale; yet, in the face of it, the thoughts of unsaved people will turn only to how their own interests are affected. This is selfishness and greed in its most naked form.

By Sea Merchants, 18:17b–19

All those connected with commerce on the seas also lament over the destruction of Babylon. This includes shipmasters, sailors, and all who travel or work in ships. Their weeping is for the same reason: their business is suddenly being destroyed. Previously, one-third of the ships will have been destroyed (8:9).

Acclaim Because of the Judgment on Babylon, 18:20–24

The reaction of the world to the destruction of Babylon, with all its business interests, has been clearly described. The people of the world weep, for material things are all they have to embrace. When these are destroyed, all is lost. The attitude that the believers ought to have toward Babylon has also been stated in verse 4. They should come out from that system and not partake of its sins. Now the reaction of heaven to the destruction of Babylon is recorded in verses 20–24.

The kings, merchants, and mariners bewail the passing of Babylon; heaven and its friends rejoice. Verse 20 declares that God has judged the case against Babylon. Babylon had slain the saints; now, God slays Babylon. Here is the final answer to the plea of the martyrs in 6:9–11. Then, as if to reassure the citizens of heaven that the destruction is final, an angel casts a millstone into the sea, symbolizing the sure and complete destruction of Babylon (v. 21).

This act brings forth a dirge concerning the total nature of the judgment on Babylon. No music, no worker, no machinery, no light, no happiness ("voice of the bridegroom and bride") shall be found in Babylon anymore. The reason is twofold: Babylon deceived the nations (v. 23), and Babylon killed the saints (v. 24).

Joyless, dark, and silent, Babylon stands as a monument to the righteous vengeance of God. Wickedness that reigned enthroned for so long is now overthrown.

EVENTS AFTER THE RAPTURE

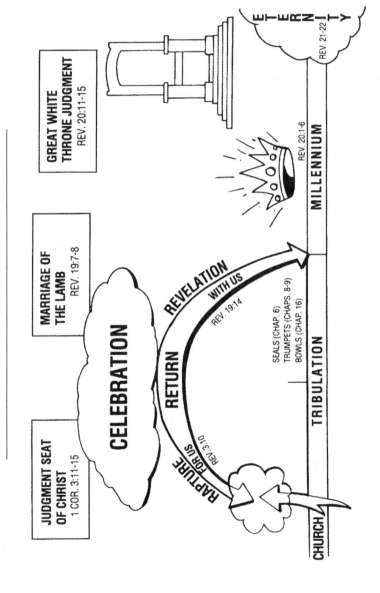

JUDGMENT SEAT OF CHRIST 1 COR. 3:11-15

MARRIAGE OF THE LAMB REV. 19:7-8

GREAT WHITE THRONE JUDGMENT REV. 20:11-15

CELEBRATION

RAPTURE FOR US
REV. 3:10

RETURN

REVELATION

WITH US
REV. 19:14

CHURCH

TRIBULATION

SEALS (CHAP. 6)
TRUMPETS (CHAPS. 8-9)
BOWLS (CHAP. 16)

MILLENNIUM
REV. 20:1-6

ETERNITY
REV. 21-22

THE SECOND COMING
OF CHRIST

19:1–21

....

Joy in Heaven, 19:1–10

The Halleujahs of the Multitude, 19:1–6

The time sequence. "After these things" evidently refers to the visions of the chapters immediately preceding. In 18:20 the call to rejoice was issued; here is the response to that call.

The group involved. The four alleluias come from "a loud voice of a great multitude in heaven" (v. 1). This is most likely the "great multitude" of 7:9–12. It does not include the twenty-four elders or the four living ones, since they are specifically distinguished in verse 4. However, nothing in the text forbids the inclusion of angels in the group, for the word translated "multitude" in verse 1 is actually the word that means "crowd" (and is the same word used in 7:9).

The content. The word "Hallelujah" occurs only in this chapter in the New Testament. In the Old Testament it is often translated "Praise the Lord," and it occurs twenty-four times in the Psalms. Here the crowd praises the Lord for four things: (1) for His redemption (v. 1); (2) for His righteous judgments, particularly on Babylon, whose punishment is eternal since her smoke rises up forever (vv. 2–3); (3) for His worth (the meaning of worship in v. 4); and (4) for His coming reign (v. 6). In the meantime, the twenty-four elders and the four living ones have joined in a hallelujah (v. 4), and a voice from heaven has called for additional praise (v. 5). The voice from the throne is not named, but it probably belongs to an angel.

The Marriage of the Lamb, 19:7–10

The announcement of the marriage, v. 7. The marriage is announced as that of the Lamb. Normally a wedding is announced in the name of the bride, but not this one. It is His marriage, and He, not the bride, will be the center of attraction. If there were a musical processional in this wedding, it would not be "Here Comes the Bride," but "Here Comes the Bridegroom!"

The array of the bride, vv. 7b–8. The delicate balance between the sovereignty of God and human responsibility is maintained in the two phrases "has made herself ready" (she did it) and "it was given to her" (God did it). The bride's array is "fine linen," which is explained as "the righteous acts of the saints." In other words, the bride's wedding garment will be made up of the righteous deeds done in life. The bride is the bride because of the righteousness of Christ; the bride is clothed for the wedding because of her acts. Righteous acts flow from a righteous character, which is entirely of the grace of God.

The accompaniment of the marriage, v. 9. The wedding is followed by a supper, and a special blessing is pronounced upon those who are called to the meal. These are the friends of the Bridegroom, and one immediately recalls John 3:29, where John the Baptist is called a friend of the Bridegroom. These guests are not the bride, and they are not unsaved people, so they must be redeemed people who are not members of the church, the body of Christ. The certainty of this beatitude is underscored by the proclamation, "These are true words of God."

The awe of John, v. 10. John seems to have been overawed by this revelation of the marriage of the Lamb, and he falls at the feet of the messenger. But he is restrained by what the messenger tells him—that he is not deity but a fellow servant; therefore, he is not to be worshiped or bowed down to. Although Christians should recognize the place of angels in carrying out the purposes of God, and consequently respect them, this verse clearly shows the impropriety of kneeling before an angel (or a representation of one). Worship belongs to God alone. "The testimony of Jesus is the spirit of prophecy" simply means that the study of prophecy should point to Jesus.

Judgment on Earth, 19:11–21

The Advent of Christ 19:11–16

His aim, v. 11. Again heaven is opened (cf. 6:14), but this time to permit the Lamb to descend to earth in His second coming. He is on a "white horse," and His name is "Faithful and True." This is particularly appropriate to the action He is about to take: judging and waging war. His purpose in coming is to put down all rebellion by war and by judgment.

His appearance, vv. 12–13. His eyes were as "a flame of fire" (1:14), denoting the penetrating quality of His judgment. On His head were "many diadems," indicating His majesty and sovereignty. Earlier in the book, Satan and Antichrist were both depicted as wearing diadems (12:3; 13:1). The name no one knew is just that, unrevealed. His robe was "dipped in blood," a striking picture since this is before He enters into battle. It is a sure token of the righteous vengeance that will shortly be displayed in battle.

He also carries the name "The Word of God." This is a title used only by John (John 1:1, 14; 1 John 1:1). Verse 16 adds another name to the list.

His armies, v. 14. His armies are apparently composed of saints, since the clothing is the same as in verse 8.

His authority, vv. 15–16. His absolute authority is demonstrated by the "sharp sword" coming out of His mouth (1:16; 2:12, 16), by his taking up the rule of the nations, in the figure of treading out the winepress (14:20), and in the name "King of kings and Lord of lords." A winepress consisted of two vats placed at different levels. The grapes were trodden in the upper vat and the juice received in the lower one (cf. 14:20). The word for "rule" (v. 15) is literally "shepherd." This shepherd will use a rod of iron on the nations of this world.

The Armageddon War, 19:17–21

The carnage, vv. 17–18. So great will be the slaughter in the war of Armageddon that an angel calls together the birds of midheaven to "eat the flesh" of those who fall in the battle. The word "midheaven" likely refers here to the space between the earth and the sky (elsewhere in 8:13 and 14:6, where it likely refers to the particular angel as being seen at the same position in the sky as the sun is at noon). The victims will include kings, commanders, mighty men, horses, riders, slaves, and free men. What an ignoble end for these people and animals.

The conflict, v. 19. The Beast and his followers, and other world leaders and their followers, assemble to make war with the Lamb. The world resists God to the bitter end.

The captives, v. 20. The two leaders, the Beast and the False Prophet (the two persons in chapter 13), are captured and cast alive into the "lake of fire which burns with brimstone." They are still there one thousand years later (20:10) and will be forever.

The conquest, v. 21. The rest were killed by the Lord. Deprived of their leaders, the people are quickly conquered. Christ's victory will be complete. Note other references to these events in Joel 3:2, 13–15; Zechariah 12:3–4, 9–10; 13:9; 14:2–8; Matthew 24:28; Luke 17:37.

THE MILLENNIUM AND THE GREAT WHITE THRONE JUDGMENT

20:1–15

....

Chapter 20 is like a great calm after the storm. In the major outline of the book, this chapter is the second part of the third main section of the book. The third section includes "the things which shall take place after these things" (chaps. 4–22). The first part of this section was the description of the tribulation period (chaps. 4–19); this second part relates to the Millennium (chap. 20), and the third part describes the eternal state (chaps. 21–22).

The Millennium, 20:1–10

"Millennium" simply means "one thousand years" and is understood as a time of peace and plenty on this earth. People hold three principal views concerning the Millennium. Some believe that the church will bring in this period during this present time between the first and second comings of Christ. Then, when the earth has experienced this peace for a long time (it does not have to be exactly a thousand years), Christ will return in His second coming. Since His return is after (post) the Millennium, this view is called postmillennialism.

Others do not believe in a Millennium at all. When Christ returns there will be a general resurrection and a general judgment and eternity will begin. This is amillennialism, for there is no (a) Millennium.

The third view is called premillennialism, since the second coming of Christ is before (pre) the Millennium. It is His return that ushers in the thousand years of peace on earth. Literal interpretation is the foundation for this view.

One of the objections often raised against premillennialism is that only Revelation 20 speaks of the time period as one thousand years (six times, however, in this one chapter). That is true, but it is also true that many other passages in the Bible describe the period (see, among many others, Ps. 110:3; Isa. 2:1–4; 11; 19:23–25; 35; 65:17–25; Jer. 23:5; Ezek. 40–48; Dan. 2:44–45, 7:23–27; Amos 9:11–15; Mic. 4:1–4; Zech. 14:3–12; Matt. 19:28; Luke 1:31–33; Acts 1:6; Rom. 11:26–27). It will be a time of unprecedented and universal peace, prosperity, and justice under the rule of Christ, the benevolent despot. In the same arena (this earth) where our Lord was seemingly defeated during His first coming, He will reign victoriously after His second coming.

Satan, 20:1–3

During this millennial age Satan will be bound and put out of action until the very end. This is certainly not true today (1 Peter 5:8). The agent that binds Satan is an angel. He is an angel to whom this authority has been given because he has the key to the Abyss and a chain (cf. 2 Peter 2:4 and Jude 6, where chains are also used to confine spirit beings). The duration of his confinement will be a thousand years. This is to be understood as literally as other numbers in the book. The purpose of his being bound is "that he would not deceive the nations any longer" (v. 3). However, at the end of that period he will be loosed "for a short time."

Saints, 20:4–6

John apparently saw three groups of saints in verse 4. He saw first those who sat on the thrones and who shared in the judging, apparently a reference to the church (cf. 1 Cor. 6:2; 2 Tim. 2:12). Then he saw a particular group of martyrs—those who were "beheaded." Literally, the word means "killed with an ax." That means of execution was practiced in ancient Rome. Finally, he saw those who had refused to worship the Beast and receive his mark. They (referring to those believers who die during the Tribulation) live and reign with Christ and share in the joys of the Millennium. The church saints will have already been raised at the Rapture, but this Tribulation group of saints will be raised at the second coming of Christ.

"The rest of the dead," that is, the unsaved dead, are not raised at this time according to verse 5. They will be raised at the conclusion of the thousand years. Therefore, clearly there is not one general resurrection as amillennialism teaches. The "first resurrection" (in several stages) includes all those who believe, since those included in the first resurrection are called "blessed" (v. 6). Over them "the second death [cf. v. 14] has no power," as it does over the unsaved dead. The Lord indicated this same distinction of two resurrections in John 5:29, but He did not specify the time interval between the two.

Sinners, 20:7–10

As predicted in verse 3, Satan will be loosed at the close of the thousand-year reign of Christ on the earth. He will find plenty of people who will follow his deception, their number being as the "sand of the seashore." "Gog and Magog" in verse 8 remind one of Ezekiel 38–39, but this is obviously not the same battle, since the time is different (Ezek. 38:16) and the judgment is dissimilar (Ezek. 38:19–22). Satan's host of followers will besiege the "camp of the saints" in Jerusalem and be put to death quickly by an act of God, which sends fire down out of heaven to devour them. Then the devil is cast into the Lake of Fire, where the Beast and False Prophet have already been for a thousand years.

Where will this large number of followers of Satan come from? In the space of a thousand years there can be thirty or forty generations of people. When the Millennium begins, people with earthly bodies will enter it, but apparently none of them will be unsaved at the very beginning. But quite soon (perhaps in the first minutes) babies will be born, and in a thousand years many children will come into the world, grow up, and live unusually long lives. All of them will be obliged to give outward allegiance to Christ, who reigns on the throne, but as in every age He will not compel them to believe in their hearts. Consequently, there will be many living who have never turned to Christ for salvation, though they have obeyed Him as Head of the government. These will seize on the chance to give expression to the rebellion of their hearts when Satan arises to be their leader in this last revolt. The Millennium will prove, among other things, that a nearly perfect earthly environment (Isa. 35) and universal knowledge of the Lord (Isa. 11:9) will not change human hearts. This must be done personally and voluntarily, and multitudes will never do that during this long period.

Great White Throne Judgment, 20:11–15

The Time

This judgment follows the close of the Millennium.

The Judge

The Judge is One "from whose presence earth and heaven" flee away. According to John 5:22, the Father has given all judgment into the hands of the Son; therefore, the Judge must be Christ. The words "before God" in some translations of verse 12 (cf. KJV) should read "before the throne" (cf. NASB and NIV) and thus constitute no contradiction.

The Subjects

Those who stand in this judgment are "the dead, the great and the small." Christians are described as the "dead in Christ" (1 Thess. 4:16), but these are the unsaved dead of all ages, wherever their bodies happened to have been disposed of. Physical death claims the body; Hades claims the souls, which do not die. All stand before Christ in this judgment.

The Basis

The basis for judgment is expressly said to be the works of these people (vv. 12–13). These are apparently contained in the books mentioned in verse 12, and the Book of Life is opened only to show that no name of anyone standing before the throne is written in it. Rejection of the Savior places people in this judgment (and excludes their names from the Book of Life), but works done during their lifetimes prove that they deserve eternal punishment. It is almost like a final act of grace for Christ to show people that, even on the basis of their own records, they deserve the Lake of Fire.

The Result

The result of this judgment is that all of those who are in it are cast into the Lake of Fire. This is "the second death"—eternal separation from God. Even death (which claims the body) and Hades (which claims the soul) are cast into the Lake of Fire, since their work is now done. The death people die on earth is only temporary. All will partake of resurrection. The prison of the soul at death, Hades, is also temporary; for the final and eternal separation, the second death, is in the Lake of Fire.

MILLENNIAL VIEWS

PREMILLENNIALISM

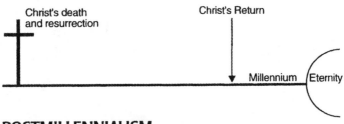

POSTMILLENNIALISM

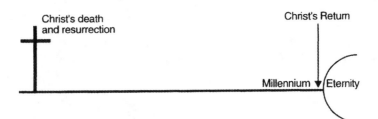

AMILLENNIALISM

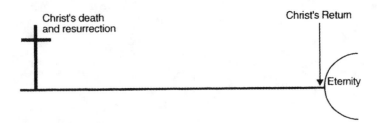

THE ETERNAL STATE

21:1–22:5

....

To review, the major outline of the book is taken from 1:19. The third section, "the things which will take place after these things," comprises chapters 4–22. That section is divided into three parts, which are in chronological order: the Tribulation (chaps. 4–19), the Millennium (chap. 20), and the eternal state (21:1–22:5).

Throughout these last two chapters of Revelation the discussion focuses on a city, the New Jerusalem. That this is the description of eternity seems apparent from the phrases in 21:1 and the close association between verses 1 and 2. Almost all commentators recognize this. Some, however, feel that the section in 21:9–21 relates the New Jerusalem to the Millennium.

At first glance this might seem incongruent with the chronological pattern of the book and of this section. Perhaps the best way to understand this entire section is to regard the New Jerusalem as the abode of the redeemed of all ages. The conditions within the New Jerusalem are those of eternity. Of course, the redeemed will inhabit the city during the Millennium, as well as during eternity. The conditions within the city are always eternal, even when the city is related to the Millennium. This is no different from the present, for believers in heaven are enjoying eternal conditions, as is God, even though these eternal conditions can also relate to time (as, for instance, on the Mount of Transfiguration or this entire vision given to John in the Revelation). In other words, the New Jerusalem is the eternal residence of the redeemed during both the Millennium and eternity. It is the place our Lord has gone to prepare for us (John 14:2).

The Descent of the City, 21:1–8

Three phrases in verse 1 underscore the fact that eternal conditions are now being described. (1) John saw "a new heaven and a new earth." The word for "new" means new in quality—"it suggests fresh life rising from the decay and wreck of the old world."[1] Both heaven and earth are included in this new creation. (2) The old had "passed away." (3) There was "no longer any sea." Whatever else this phrase may mean, it seems to indicate clearly the end of the old order (Ex. 20:11; Ezek. 48:28) and a complete change in climatic conditions.

John then saw the New Jerusalem. The writer to the Hebrews speaks of this heavenly Jerusalem as the abode of the saints (Heb. 12:22–24). John identifies it as the "bride" (v. 2). The city comes "down out of heaven" to give accessibility to the earth, but this does not mean that conditions within the city are earthly.

The first characteristic of the new condition is that God is with people, v. 3. God Himself will "dwell" (literally, "tabernacle"; cf. John 1:14) with people during eternity.

Old experiences will be eliminated, vv. 4–5. God will "wipe away every tear." Death will vanish and with it sorrow, crying, and pain. These negatives are summarized in a positive statement in verse 5: "Behold, I am making all things new." Then John is instructed by God, who sits on the throne, to write, for the "words are faithful and true." John was probably so overwhelmed at what he was seeing and learning that he forgot momentarily to write (cf. 14:13; 19:9).

New things will be experienced, vv. 6–7. First, a complete satisfaction ("the spring of the water of life"); second, a full inheritance (v. 7a); and, third, full fellowship (v. 7b) will be the reward of God's people.

Certain people will be excluded, v. 8. People who are characterized by any of the eight traits listed here will be in the Lake of Fire and, thus, excluded from heaven. Notice that the text does not say that anyone who has ever committed any of these sins will be excluded, but people whose lives are characterized in these ways. There is a difference, for instance, between occurrences of lying in one's life and living a liar's lifestyle. The sinful people described here are unsaved people who will be cast forever into the Lake of Fire.

The Description of the City, 21:9–27

One of the angels who poured out the bowl judgments now bids John to view the city in greater detail. His vantage point is outside the city on a high mountain. Again, the city is identified as the bride of Christ (v. 9), the place He is now preparing for His people (John 14:2). This section describes the city's relation to the millennial state. In other words, there seem to be two descents of the city, verses 21:1–8 being the one related to eternity, and 21:9–22:5 the one related to the Millennium.

Its Glory, 21:11

The glory of the city is the "glory of God." Its light is the radiance of God's complete character. Its brilliance was like that of a "very costly stone," like that of a "crystal-clear jasper," with its gorgeous hues and transparency.

167

Its Construction, 21:12–14

The city had a "great and high wall," suggesting the security of the bride. In the wall are "twelve gates" with an angel at each one (cf. Heb. 12:22), and the names of the "twelve tribes of Israel" are inscribed on them. There are three gates on each of the four sides. The wall has "twelve foundation stones," and on them are the names of the "twelve apostles." Notice that even in eternity Israel and the church are distinguished, though both are included in God's redeemed people.

Its Measurements, 21:15–17

The angel that talked with John had a "gold measuring rod" (ten feet long) to measure the city, gates, and wall. Nothing further is said about the gates, but the city measures "fifteen hundred miles," and it is in the shape of a cube, foursquare. This is about the distance from Canada to the Gulf of Mexico, or from the Atlantic Ocean to Colorado. The cube, or foursquare shape of the city, reminds one of the fourfold dimensions given of the love of God (Eph. 3:18). The wall measures "seventy-two yards" (144 cubits or 216 feet high), and these measurements by the angel are the same as "human measurements." Whether this measures the height or thickness of the wall is not clear.

Concerning the foursquare shape of the city, Swete has a worthwhile comment:

> The tetragon occurs more than once in the legislation of Exodus. Both the altar of burnt offering and the altar of incense were of this form (Ex. xxvii.l, xxx.2), and so was the High Priest's breast plate (ib.xxviii.16, xxxvi.16–xxxix.9); the feature reappears in Ezekiel's new city and temple (Ez. xli.21, xliii.16, xlv.l, xlviii.20.) In Solomon's Temple the Holy of

Holies was a perfect cube, 20 cubits each way. . . . In ancient cities the foursquare form was not unusual. . . . As is well known, the rectangular tetragon was to Greek thinkers a symbol of perfection.[2]

Henry Morris makes some intriguing observations about the city and its population. He suggests that the city will include both horizontal and vertical avenues and that the city blocks could be cubical blocks rather than square blocks as in our present-day cities. He also estimates that the total population of the world, past, present, and future, will be about one hundred billion. If 20 percent ultimately become residents of the New Jerusalem, then the city will have to accommodate twenty billion people. If residences occupy 25 percent of the space in the city (leaving 75 percent for avenues, parks, public buildings, and other areas), then each residence, or cubical block, would be about one-third of a mile on each face of the cube. Compare one-third of a mile, or 1,760 feet, to the width and depth of lots (which might range anywhere from 60 to 250 feet) on which homes are typically built today.[3] Obviously, there will be more than ample room for all who will live in the New Jerusalem.

Its Materials, 21:18–21

The wall was of "jasper" (usually green quartz) and the city of "pure gold"—both clear as crystal. The foundation was "adorned" (a word from which we derive the English word "cosmetics") with precious stones. The colors are as follows: jasper, green; sapphire, blue; chalcedony, green; emerald, green; sardonyx, brown and white; sardius, red; chrysolite, yellow; beryl, green; topaz, yellow; chrysoprase, apple green; jacinth, blue; and amethyst, purple. The gates were each "a single pearl," and the street was pure, transparent gold. From this description of heaven, our earthly minds certainly can comprehend that it is a place of extreme beauty.

Its Relation to God, 21:22–23

The city does not require a temple or a place of worship to provide access to God simply because God and the Lamb are actually present and themselves constitute the temple. The city requires no sun or moon since the glory of God and the Lamb will light the city. This does not necessarily mean that there will be no sun or moon (which may still furnish light for outlying areas), but only that they will not be required for light within the city.

Its Relation to Nations, 21:24–27

Nations and kings on the earth will bring glory and honor to the city. Several suggestions have been made concerning the involvement of "nations" here. (1) Some feel that the mention of nations shows that the time referred to reverts back to the Millennium and that John is viewing the relation of the New Jerusalem, which is suspended over the earth during the Millennium, to the people on the earth during that time. (2) Others translate (legitimately) the word "nations" as "Gentiles" and understand that saved Gentiles are simply being delineated as belonging to the New Jerusalem and bringing glory and honor into it. (3) Morris suggests that the redeemed will not only have their residences in the New Jerusalem but will also be organized with national boundaries on the new earth over which they will have jurisdiction.[4] However, entrance into the city is clearly restricted to those who are redeemed (v. 27).

The Delights of the City, 22:1–5

Fullness of Life and Blessing, 22:1–2

The source of the river is "the throne of God and of the Lamb," and, like the city, it is "clear as crystal." The river is the "water of life," and its presence in the city simply means that fullness of life will be the experience of all those who inhabit it. The "tree of life" (v. 2; cf. Gen. 2:9; Rev. 2:7) is also an assurance of fullness of life in that city. The tree yields fruit constantly, indicating the continuous blessing that will pour forth. Its leaves are for the "healing of the nations," which again indicates blessing of some sort. Since there is no more curse (v. 3), what is meant by healing the nations? The word "healing" also has the meaning of "caring for." Thus, the phrase may well mean that the leaves of the tree enhance the quality of life in a positive way, not that they heal illnesses; for there will be no illnesses when there is no longer any curse.

Fullness of Paradise, 22:3–5

Paradise excludes the curse (v. 3) and all darkness (v. 5). Paradise includes the privilege of serving God and the Lamb (v. 3), of seeing His face, and of having His name on our foreheads—a proof of complete devotion to God's service. The word for "serve" is *latreuō,* a priestly service. Paradise is not only the absence of evil but the privilege of serving God in His presence forever. It also means reigning with Him forever and ever. This is complete exaltation and perfect exultation.

THE END OF TIME

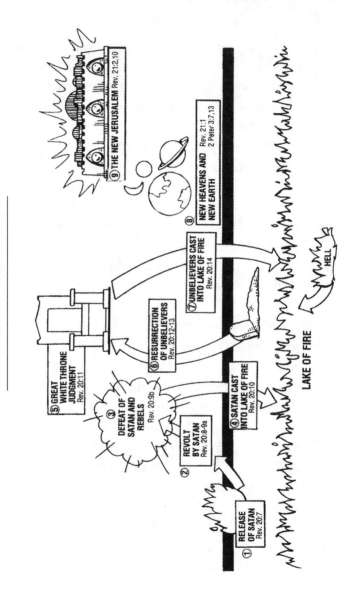

EPILOGUE

22:6–21

....

The epilogue to the book comprises most of chapter 22. It consists of words of comfort and words of caution.

Words of Comfort, 22:6–17
"These Words Are Faithful and True," 22:6

Elsewhere in the book there have been solemn affirmations of the veracity of the prophecies (15:3; 16:7; 19:2). The remainder of verse 6 is like 1:1. "Shortly" may mean that the events recorded in the book, once begun, will transpire quickly. Or it may indicate that the events are imminent. Or it may assure us of God's readiness to fulfill the promises of the book.[1]

"I Am Coming Quickly," 22:7

This reminder of the imminency of the Lord's coming is accompanied by a promise of blessing for those who keep the sayings of the book. This, too, is like the beginning of the book (1:3).

God Is the One Who Is Worthy of Worship, 22:8–9

Again John, overawed, bows down at the feet of the revealing angel "to worship" him (as in 19:10). Again, he is reprimanded and reminded that God is the One to be worshiped. The angel takes his place with the fellow servants and prophets as a creature of God and, therefore, is not to be worshiped.

The Book Is Not Sealed, 22:10–11

The book is not to be sealed since "the time is near," and people will need to understand what God is doing (cf. Dan. 12:4). When the time is fulfilled, that is, when Christ comes, destinies will be fixed. This is the meaning of verse 11. The unjust and filthy will remain this way forever, as will the righteous and holy.

Rewards Will Be Given, 22:12–13

Verse 12 includes the second occurrence of the words "Behold, I am coming quickly." But this time the assurance of His giving rewards is added. Salvation is entirely of grace, but rewards are based on works (1 Cor. 3:11–15). This is certified by the One who is Alpha and Omega (cf. 1:8, 17; 2:8).

Blessed Are the Redeemed, 22:14–15

"Blessed" marks off the last of seven beatitudes in this book (cf. 1:3; 14:13; 16:15; 19:9; 20:6; 22:7). Blessed are the redeemed who will have "the right to the tree of life" (eternal life) and entrance into the joys of the New Jerusalem. Those who have not washed their robes in the blood of the Lamb are described as "outside." The list of sinners who must suffer eternally is like the one in 21:8. Their sins are practiced currently and with more and more tolerance. "Dogs" does not refer to animals but to undesirable people (cf. Isa. 56:10–11; Phil. 3:2).

Gracious Is Our Lord, 22:16–17

(1) He is gracious because He is the One who sent His angel to reveal these things to John and the churches. How much greater

is our understanding and how different our perspective simply because the Lord chose to reveal these things about the future. (2) He is gracious because He is the root of David and thus the One who guarantees the fulfillment of all of Israel's covenantal promises. (3) He is gracious because He is the "bright morning star," assuring that a new day will dawn. (4) He is gracious because He still offers grace to anyone who will come to drink of "the water of life" freely (v. 17). "The Spirit and the bride" join in this call to the unsaved.

Words of Warning, 22:18–19
About Adding to the Book, 22:18

If anyone adds to the words of the prophecy, God will add to that person the many and varied plagues written in it (cf. Deut. 4:2; Prov. 30:6). What particular plague or plagues may be experienced in individual cases is not stated, but those who add to the book will suffer.

About Subtracting from the Book, 22:19

Subtraction proves that the individual deserves exclusion from the Book of Life, the holy city, and the promises and blessings of this prophecy. This can only mean the Lake of Fire, for all who are not written in the Book of Life are cast into that place. These are solemn warnings against ignoring, perverting, or tampering with the message of the book.

Closing Benediction, 22:20–21

For the third time in this chapter (vv. 7, 12) the Lord says that He will come quickly. John's reply is, "Come, Lord Jesus." John concludes with the customary benediction, "The grace of the Lord Jesus be with all. Amen."

NOTES

....

Introduction

1. lrenaeus, *Adversus Haereses (Against Heresies),* 5.30.3.

Chapter 3: The Seven Churches

1. J. B. Smith, *A Revelation of Jesus Christ* (Scottdale, PA: Herald, 1961), 61.

Chapter 4: The Throne in Heaven

1. Henry Barclay Swete, *The Apocalypse of St. John* (London: Macmillan, 1907), 70.

2. Lehman Strauss, *The Book of the Revelation* (Neptune, NJ: Loizeaux, 1964), 134.

3. W. R. Newell, *The Book of Revelation* (Chicago: Moody, n.d.), 373–74.

4. J. B. Smith, *A Revelation of Jesus Christ* (Scottdale, PA: Herald, 1961), 106.

Chapter 6: The Six Seals

For a demonstration of the validity of the view that the trumpets do not recapitulate the bowls and that the trumpets and bowls do not recapitulate the seals, see Wilbur M. Smith, "Revelation," in *The Wycliffe Bible Commentary* (Chicago: Moody, 1962), 1516.

Chapter 7: The Redeemed of the Tribulation

1. J. A. Seiss, *The Apocalypse* (Grand Rapids: Zondervan, 1965), 1:405–6.

2. J. B. Smith, *A Revelation of Jesus Christ* (Scottdale, PA: Herald, 1961), 135.

Chapter 8: The Seventh Seal and the First Four Trumpets

1. J. B. Smith, *A Revelation of Jesus Christ* (Scottdale, PA: Herald, 1961), 136.

2. Walter Scott, *Exposition of the Revelation of Jesus Christ* (London: Pickering & Inglis, n.d.), 180.

3. W. R. Newell, *The Book of Revelation* (Chicago: Moody, n.d.), 121.

4. Scott, *Revelation of Jesus Christ,* 184–85.

5. Henry M. Morris, *The Revelation Record* (San Diego: Creation-Life, 1983), 1340.

6. J. D. Douglas, ed., *The New Bible Dictionary* (Grand Rapids: Eerdmans, 1962), 148.

7. Newell, *Book of Revelation,* 127.

Chapter 9: Woes on the Earth

1. J. A. Seiss, *The Apocalypse* (Grand Rapids: Zondervan, 1965), 2:83.

Chapter 10: The Angel and the Little Opened Book

1. W. F. Arndt and F. W. Gingrich, eds., *A Greek-English Lexicon* (Chicago: Univ. of Chicago Press, 1957), 896.

2. W. R. Newell, *The Book of Revelation* (Chicago: Moody, n.d.), 143.

3. J. B. Smith, *A Revelation of Jesus Christ* (Scottdale, PA: Herald, 1961), 162.

4. Henry Barclay Swete, *The Apocalypse of St. John* (London: Macmillan, 1907), 132.

Chapter 11: The Temple, the Two Witnesses, and the Seventh Trumpet

1. Seiss, *The Apocalypse,* 235–36.

Chapter 16: The Seven Bowl Judgments

1. Henry Barclay Swete, *The Apocalypse of St. John* (London: Macmillan, 1907), 201.

2. Henry M. Morris, *The Revelation Record* (San Diego: Creation-Life, 1983), 303–304.

Chapter 17: Religious Babylon

1. Henry Barclay Swete, *The Apocalypse of St. John* (London: Macmillan, 1907), 220.

Chapter 21: The Eternal State

1. Henry Barclay Swete, *The Apocalypse of St. John* (London: Macmillan, 1907), 275.

2. Ibid., 284.

3. Henry M. Morris, *The Revelation Record* (San Diego: Creation-Life, 1983), 451.

4. Ibid., 459.

Chapter 22: Epilogue

1. William H. Simcox, *The Revelation* (Cambridge: Cambridge Univ. Press, 1893), 40.

SOME HELPFUL COMMENTARIES ON REVELATION

Criswell, W. A. *Expository Sermons on Revelation.* 5 vols. Grand Rapids: Zondervan, 1962–1966. These are not only excellent expository sermons, but they contain careful exegesis. The viewpoint is premillennial and pretribulational.

Morris, Henry M. *The Revelation Record.* San Diego: Creation-Life, 1983. Fine commentary with excellent scientific insights about the Tribulation judgments.

Newell, William R. *The Book of the Revelation.* Chicago: Moody, 1935. Consistently literal in interpretation. Very helpful appendices.

Scott, Walter. *Exposition of the Revelation of Jesus Christ.* London: Pickering & Inglis, n.d. This is the fountainhead of all the subsequent "Plymouth Brethren" commentaries. It is very thorough and helpful.

Seiss, J. A. *The Apocalypse.* Grand Rapids: Zondervan, 1865. This older commentary is still very helpful.

Smith, J. B. *A Revelation of Jesus Christ.* Scottsdale, PA: Herald, 1961. The author, a Mennonite, has written a detailed exegesis of Revelation from the pretribulational, premillennial viewpoint. Many statistics and comparisons are included.

Smith, Wilbur M. "Revelation." In *The Wycliffe Bible Commentary*. Chicago: Moody, 1962. A very useful and reliable commentary.

Strauss, Lehman. *The Book of the Revelation*. Neptune, NJ: Loizeaux, 1964. An excellent, popular work.

Swete, Henry Barclay. *The Apocalypse of St. John*. London: Macmillan, 1907. Helpful for Greek exegesis, but not futuristic in viewpoint.

Walvoord, John F. *The Revelation of Jesus Christ*. Chicago: Moody, 1966. Careful and detailed exegesis from the pretribulation, premillennial viewpoint.

STUDY THE BIBLE WITH PROFESSORS FROM MOODY BIBLE INSTITUTE

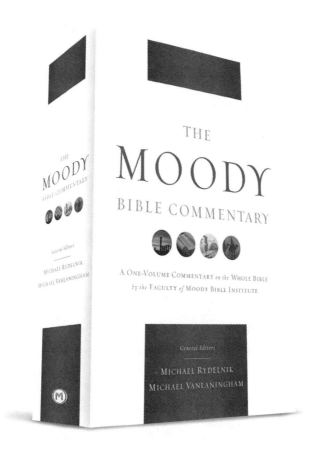

DIG DEEP INTO THE
WHOLE NEW TESTAMENT!

MacArthur New Testament Commentary Series

The set includes:

Matthew (4 volumes)	Galatians	Hebrews
Mark (2 volumes)	Ephesians	James
Luke (4 volumes)	Philippians	1 Peter
John (2 volumes)	Colossians & Philemon	2 Peter and Jude
Acts (2 volumes)	1 & 2 Thessalonians	1-3 John
Romans (2 volumes)	1 Timothy	Revelation (2 volumes)
1 Corinthians	2 Timothy	Index
2 Corinthians	Titus	

MOODY
Publishers®

From the Word to Life®

This bestselling 34-volume hardcover commentary set features verse-by-verse interpretation and rich application of God's Word. Easy to understand, yet rich in scholarly background.

978-0-8024-1347-5 | also available as an eBook

ENCOUNTER GOD. WORSHIP MORE.

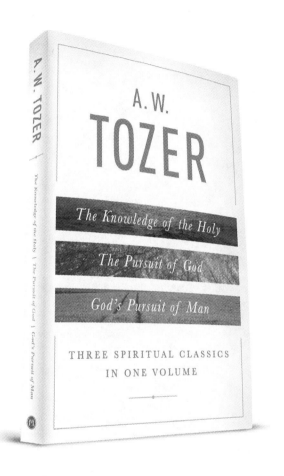

MOODY Publishers®

From the Word to Life®

Considered to be Tozer's greatest works, *The Knowledge of the Holy*, *The Pursuit of God*, and *God's Pursuit of Man* are now available in a single volume. In *Three Spiritual Classics*, you will discover a God of breathtaking majesty and world-changing love, and you will find yourself worshipping through every page.

978-0-8024-1861-6